Drawing Heroes, Villains, and Pets with Melvin and Me

Written and Illustrated by
Shawn Durington

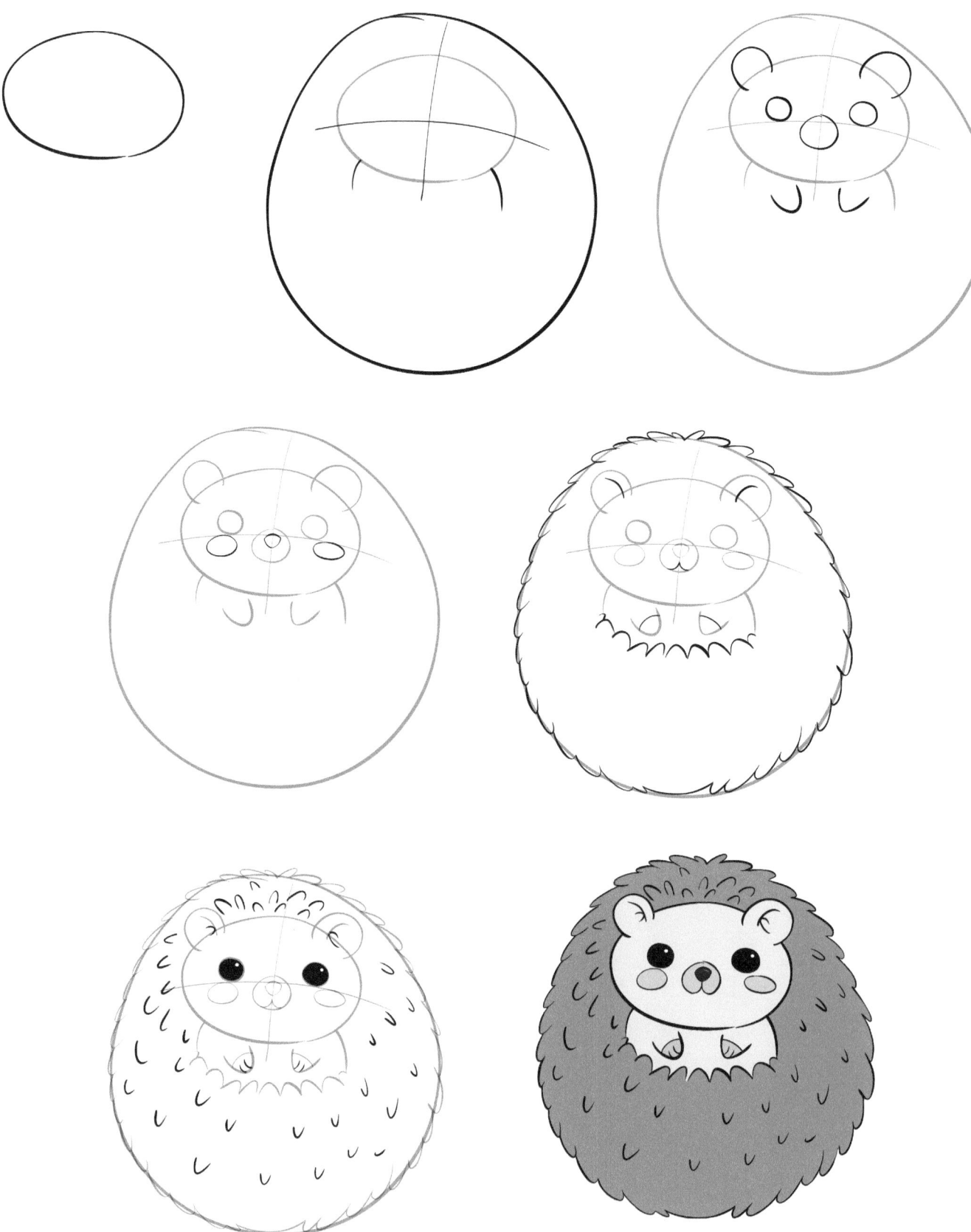

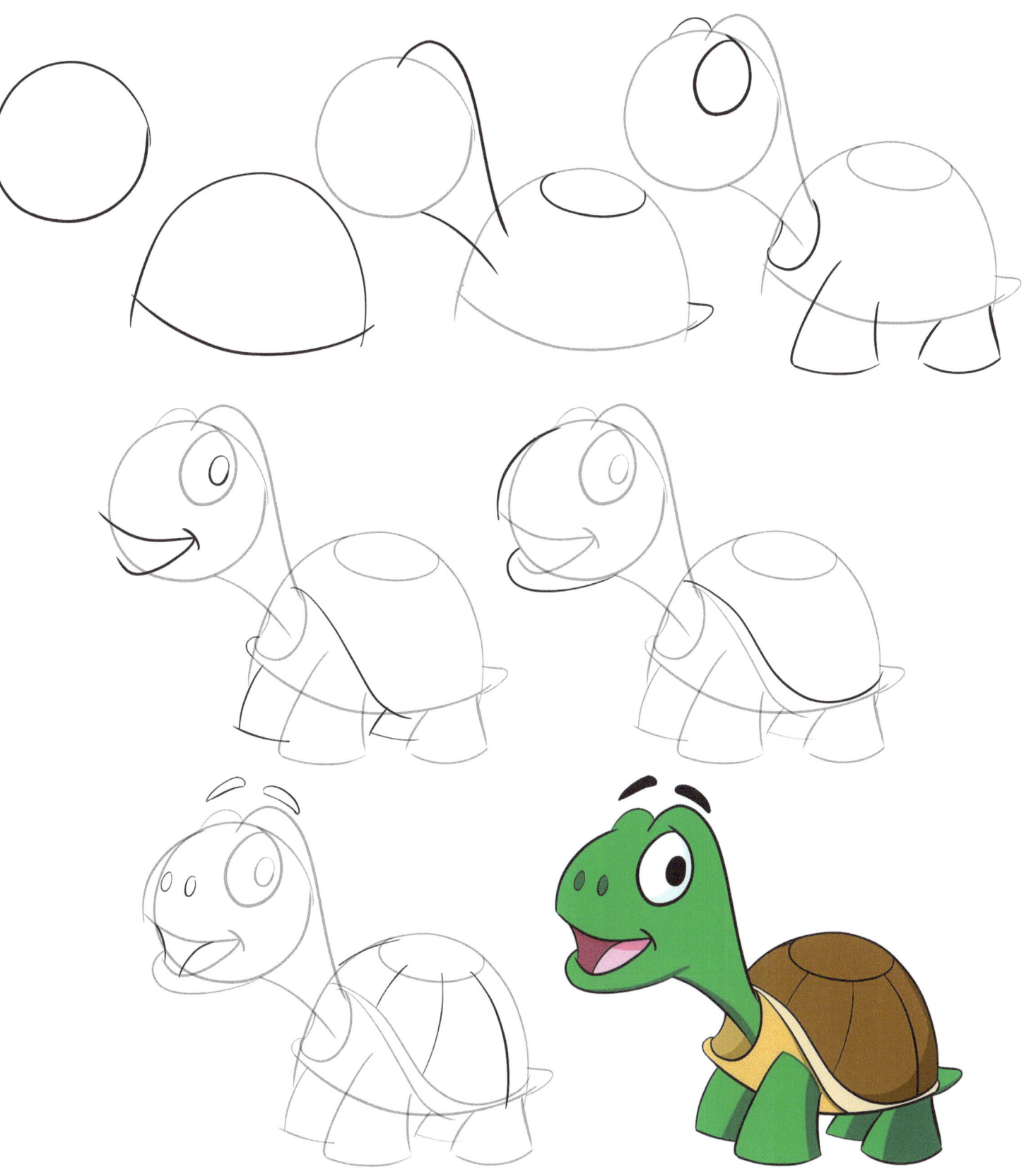

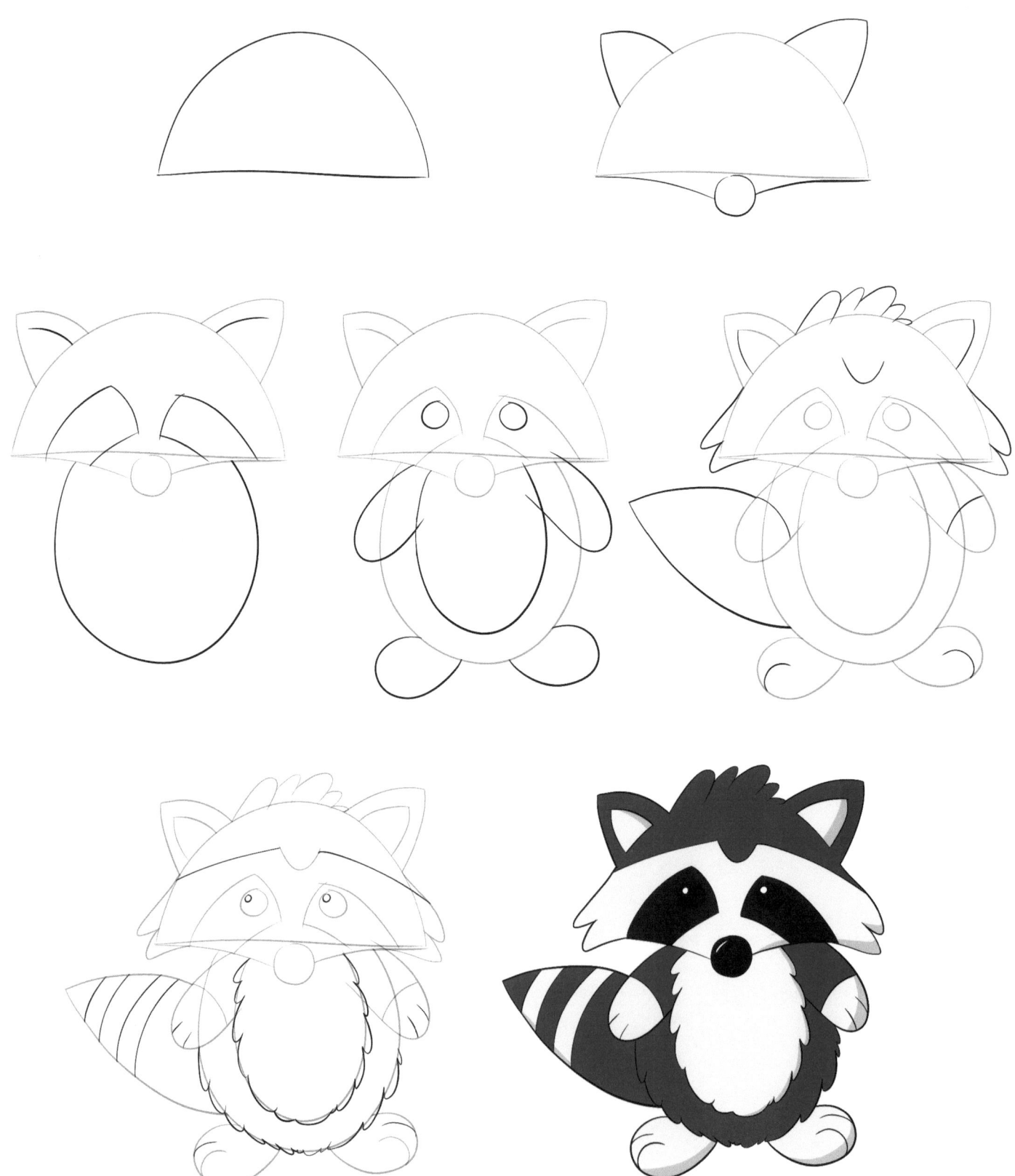

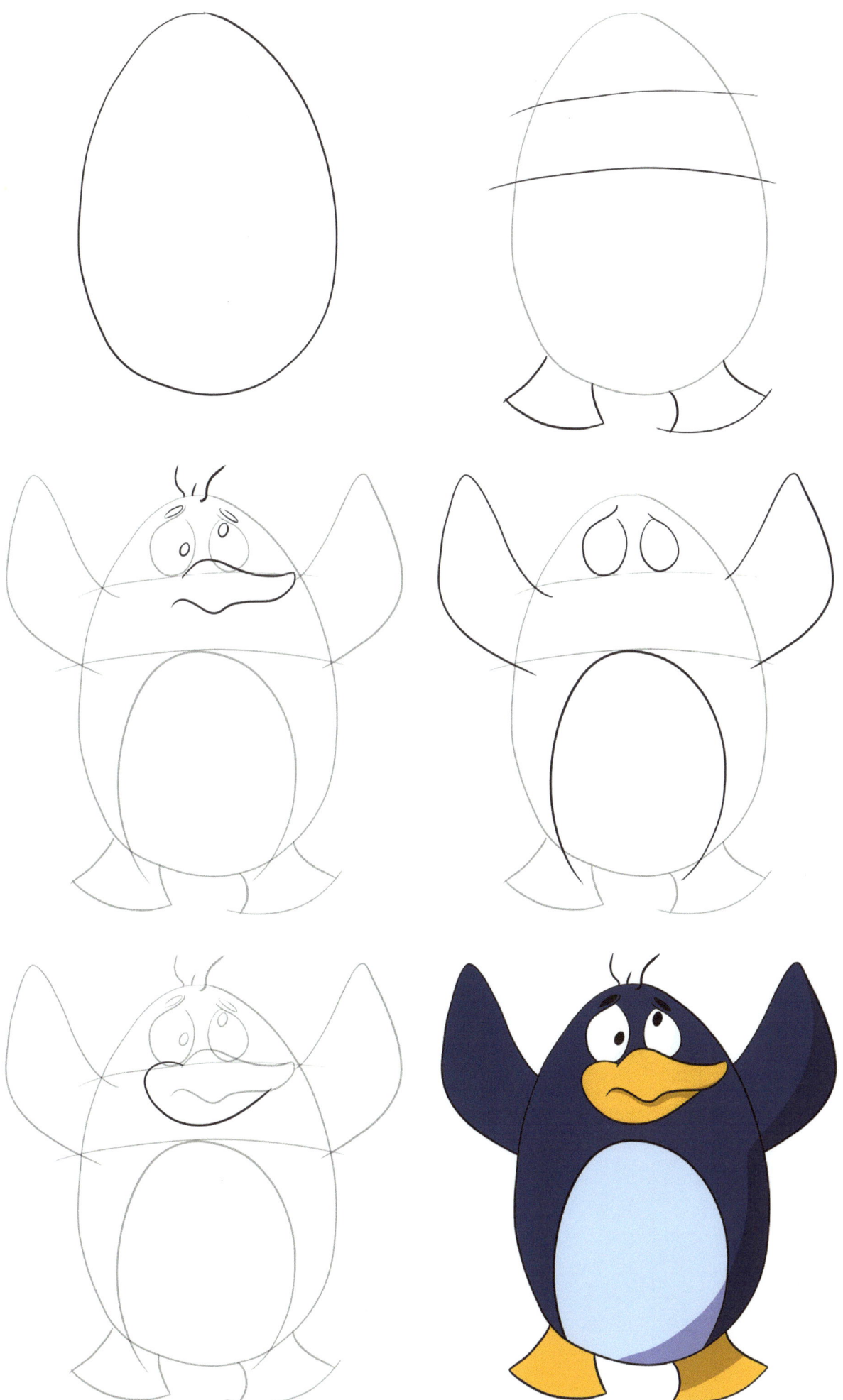

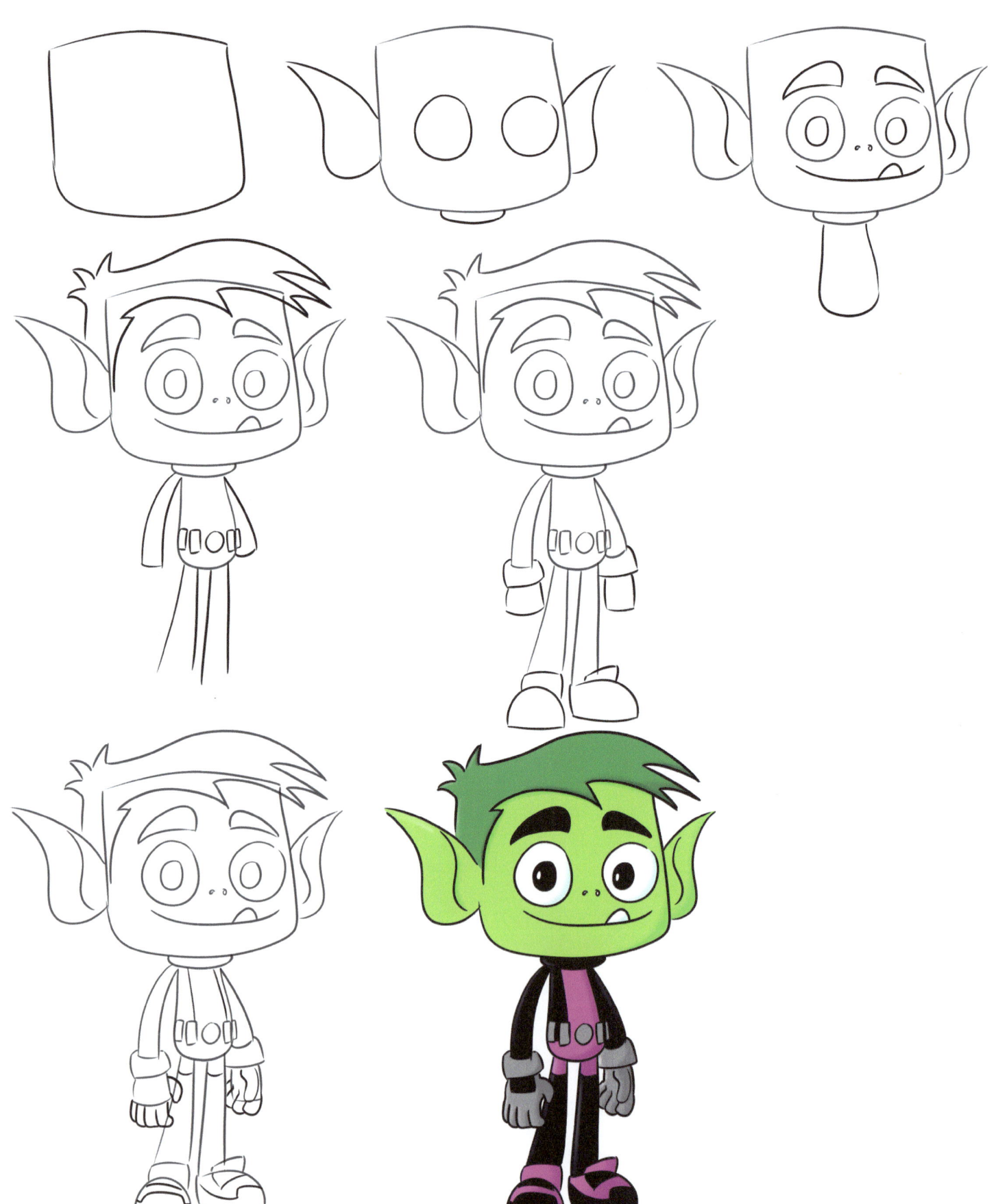

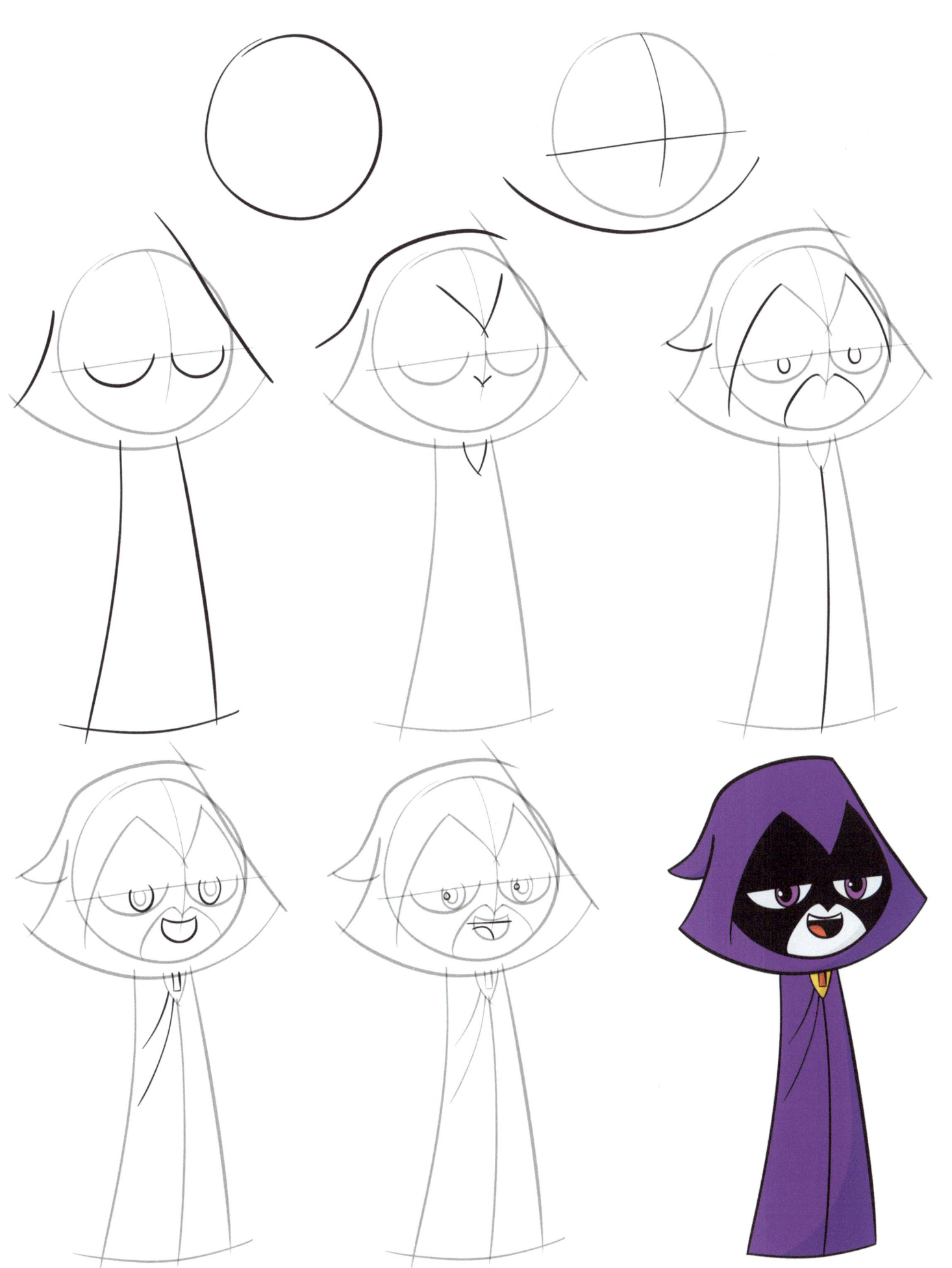

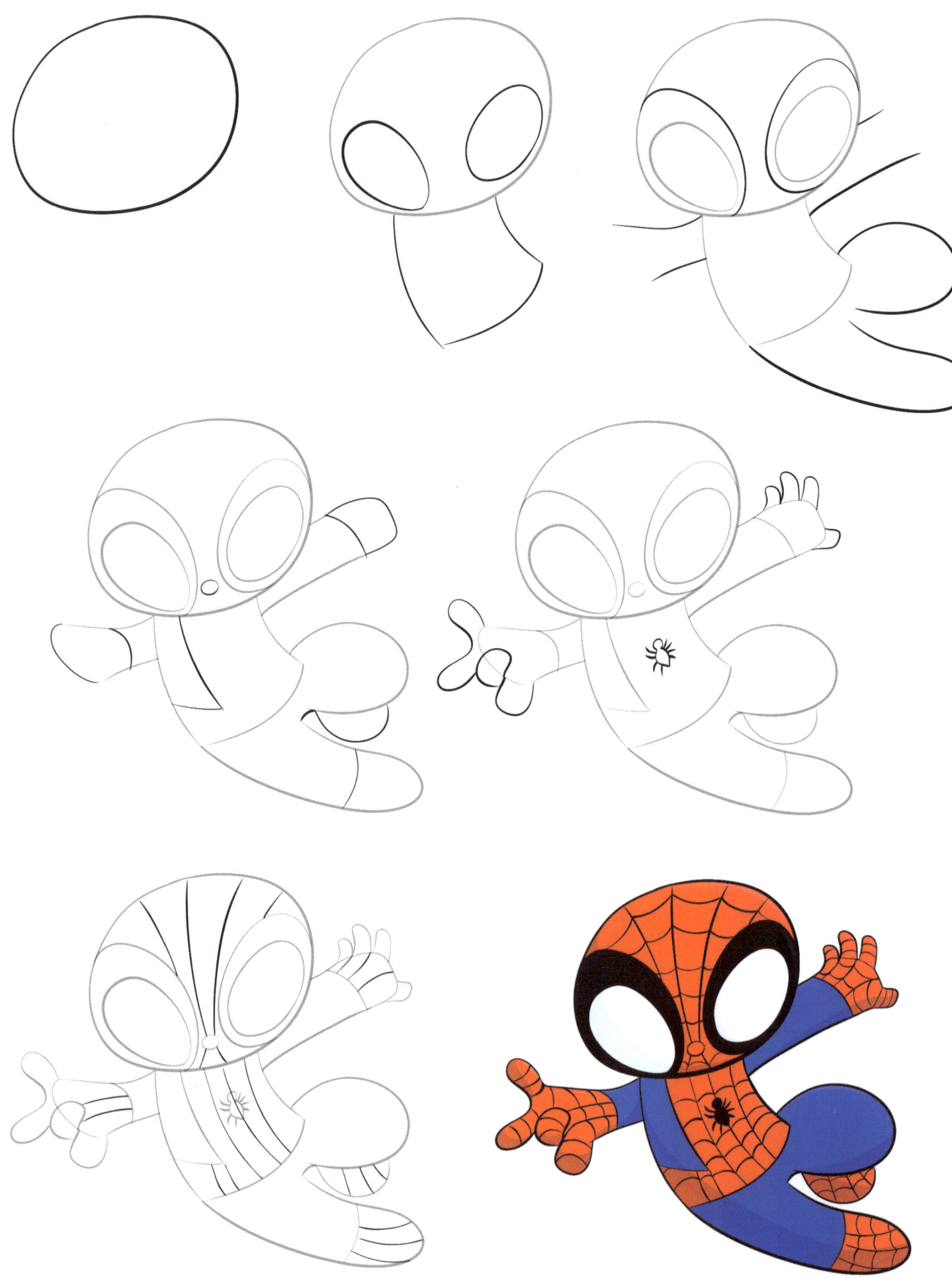

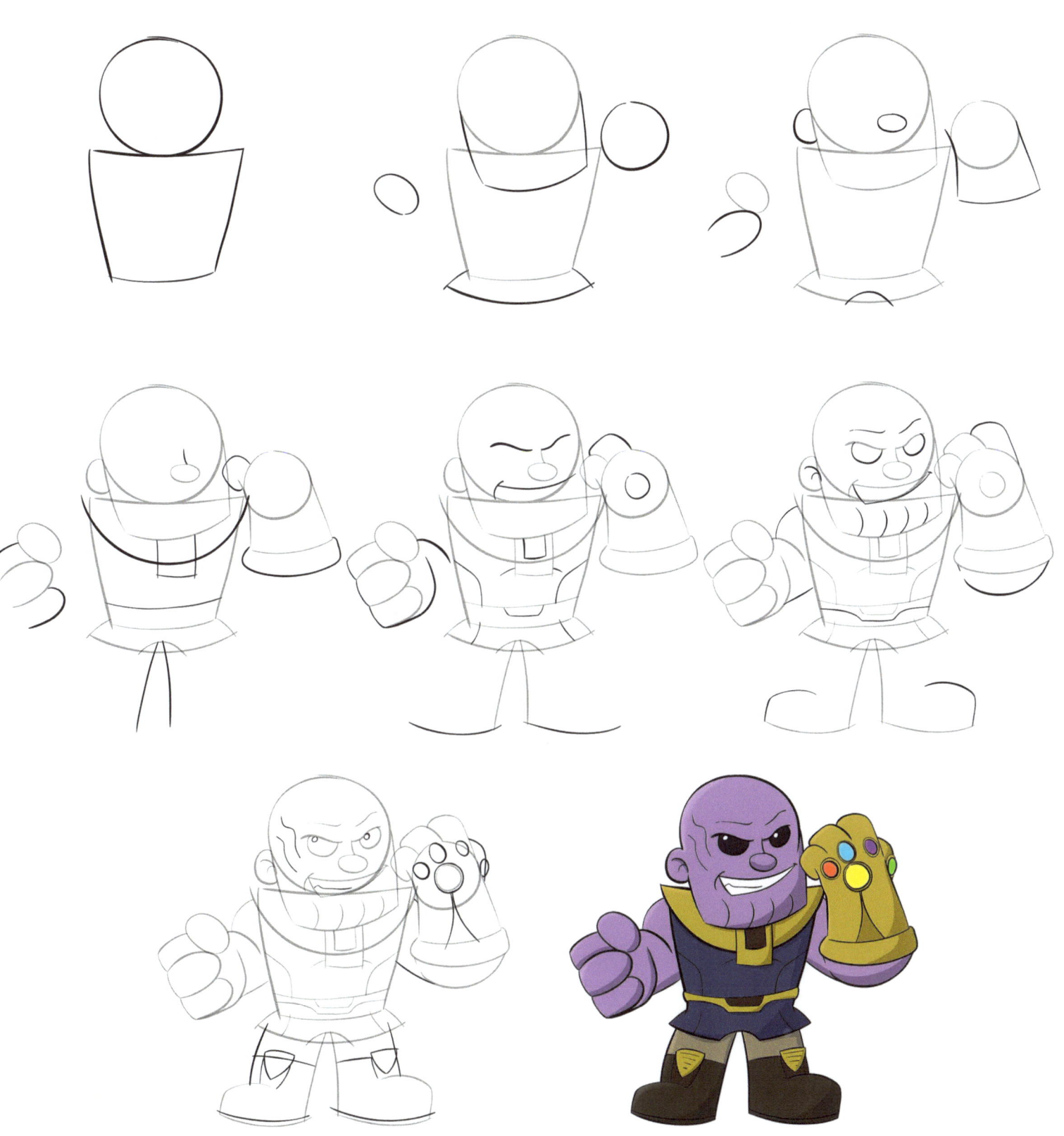

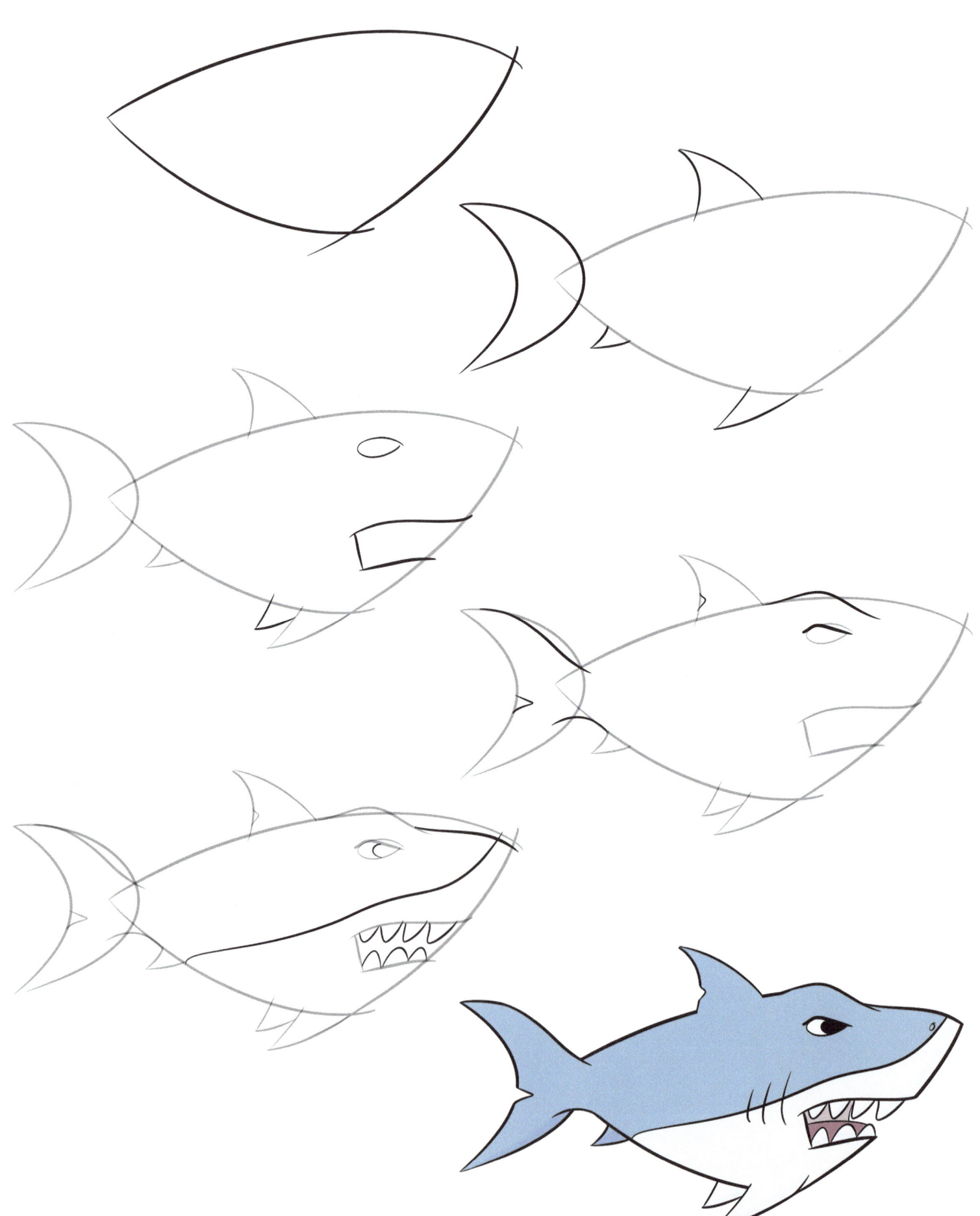

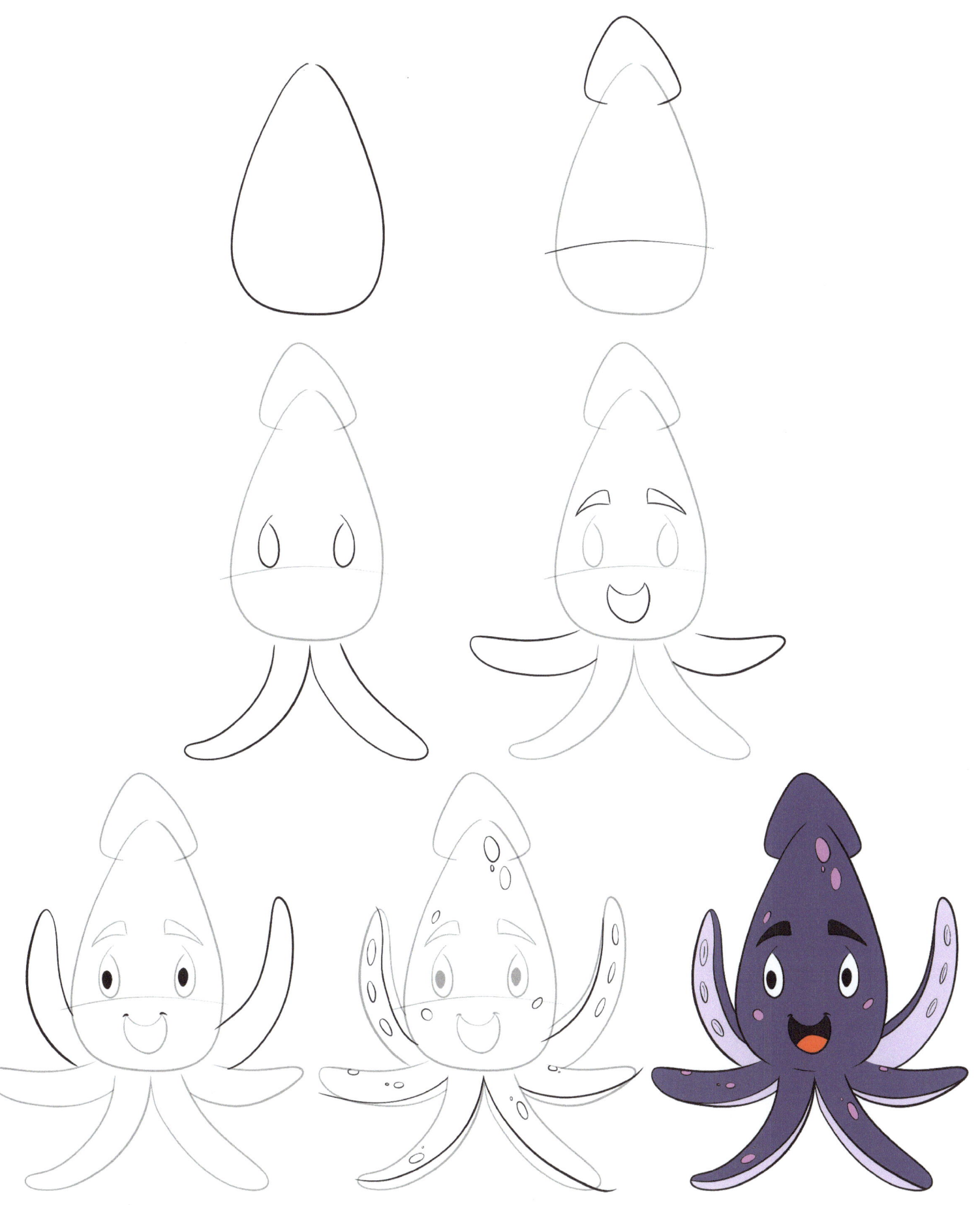

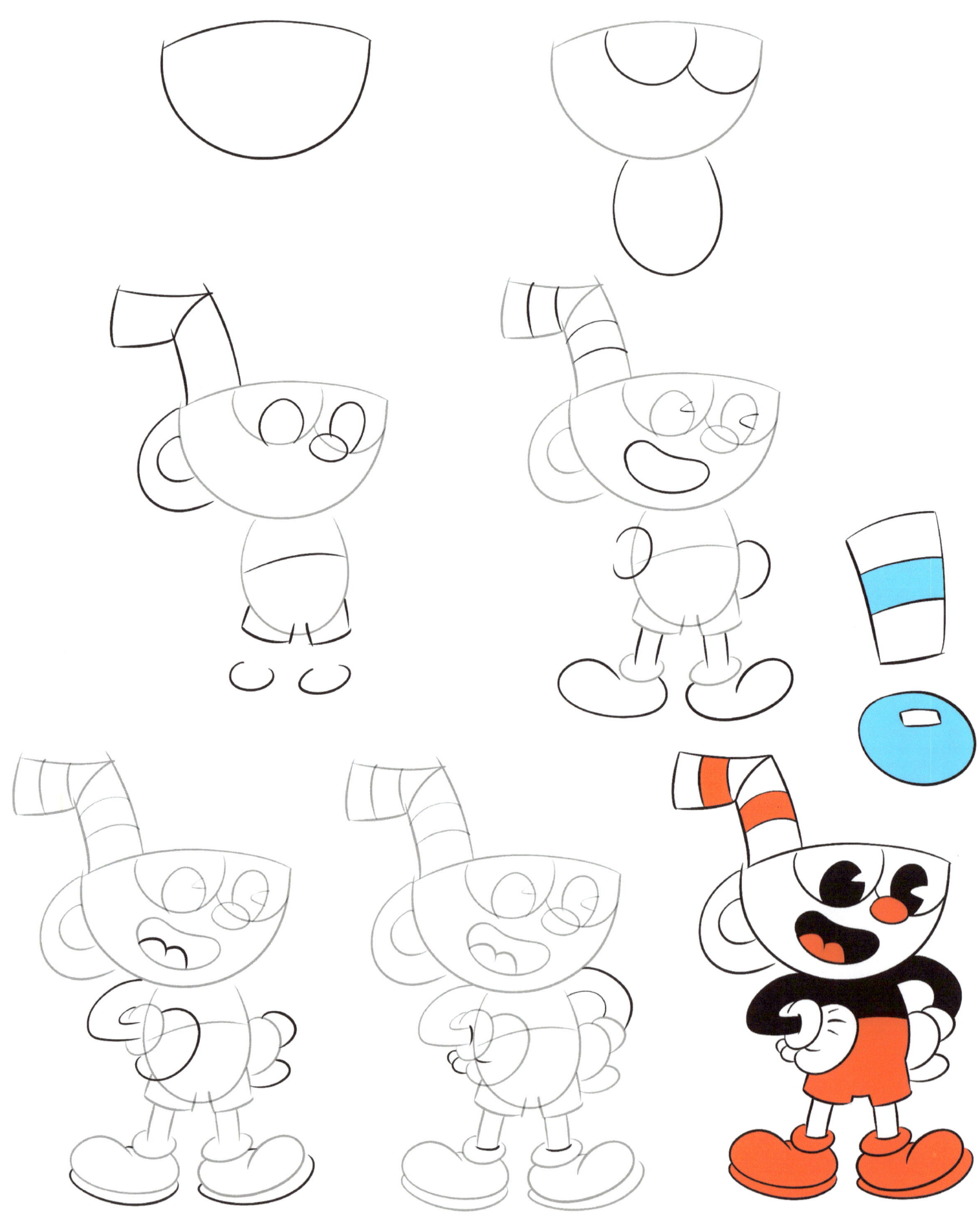

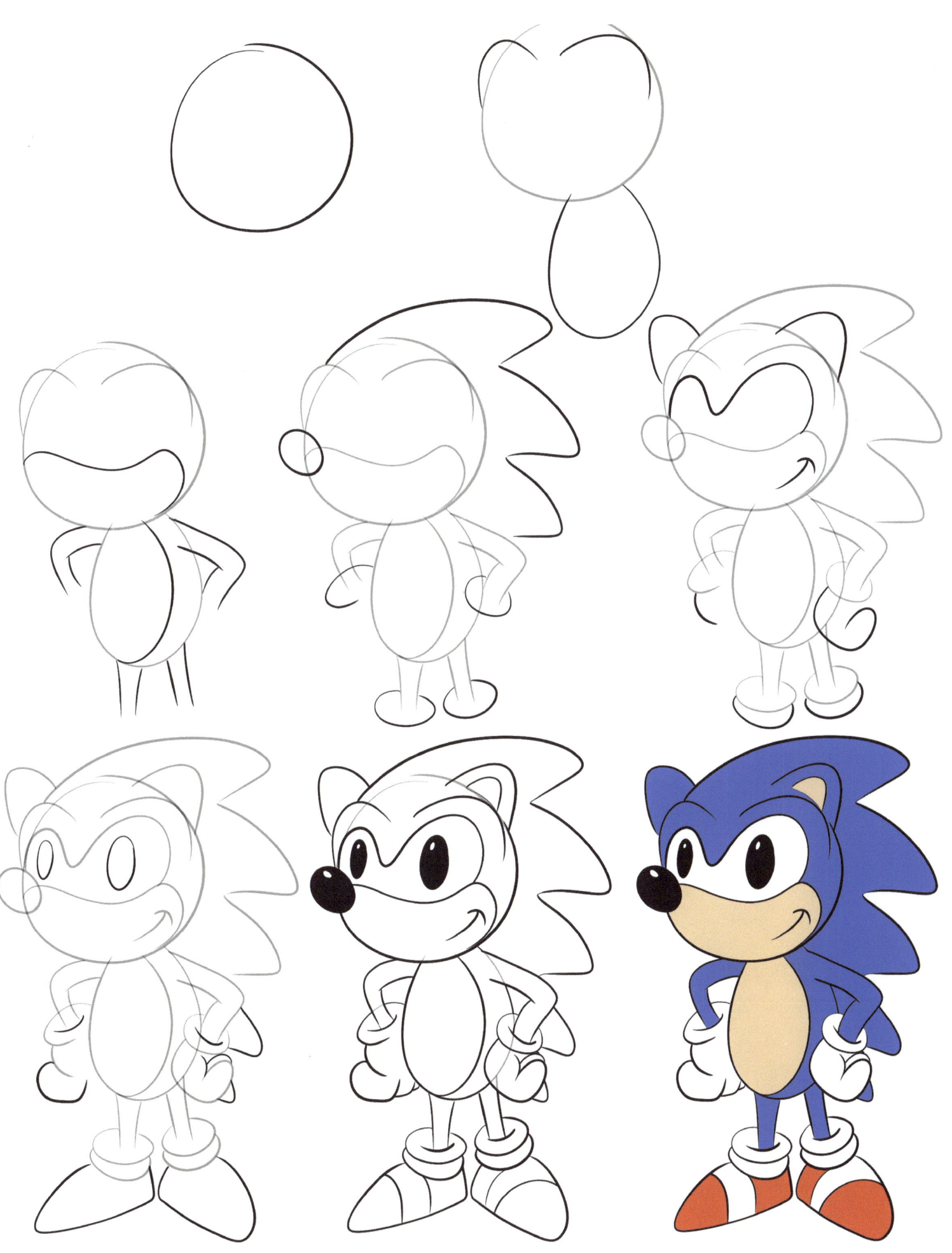

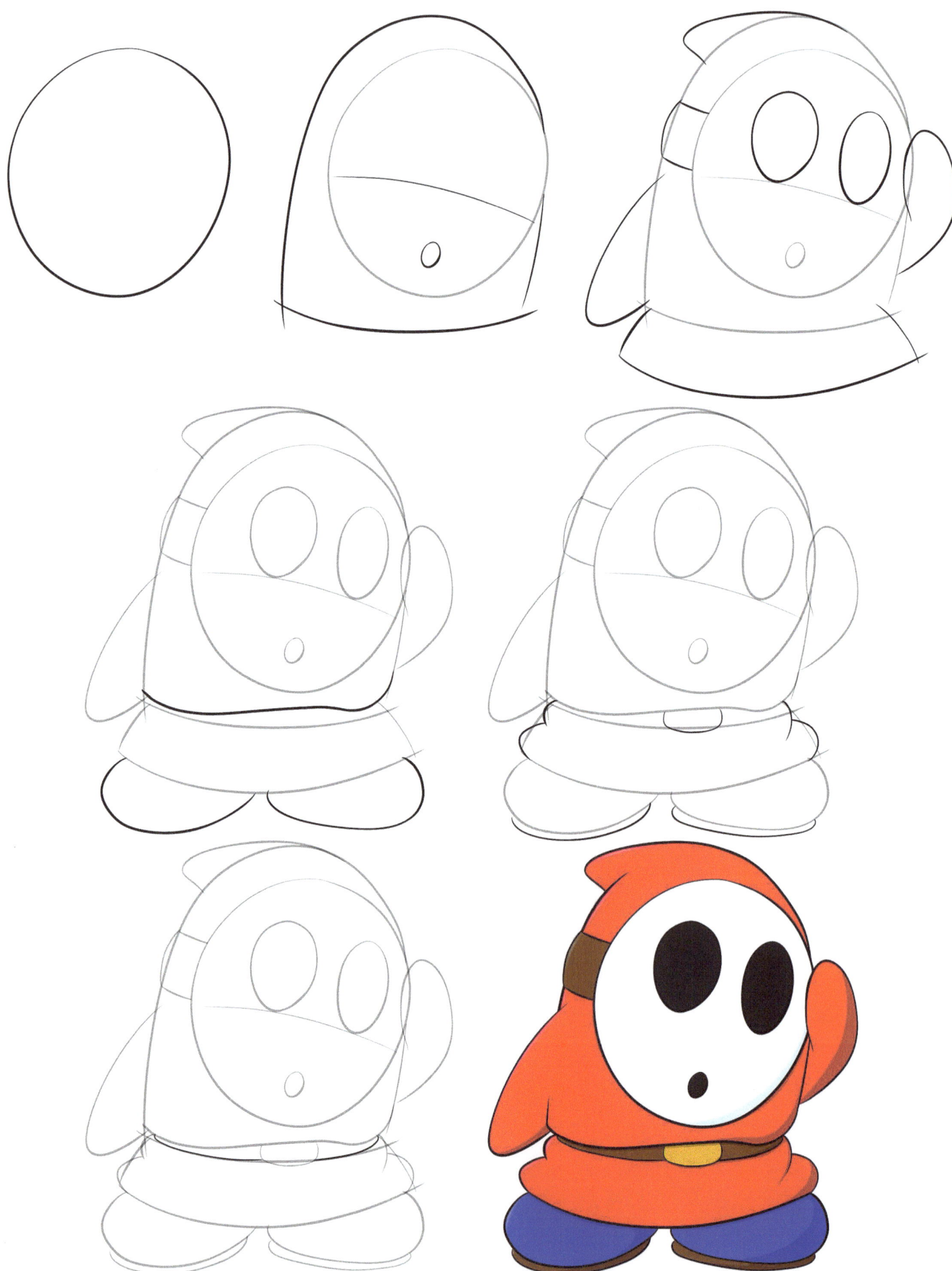

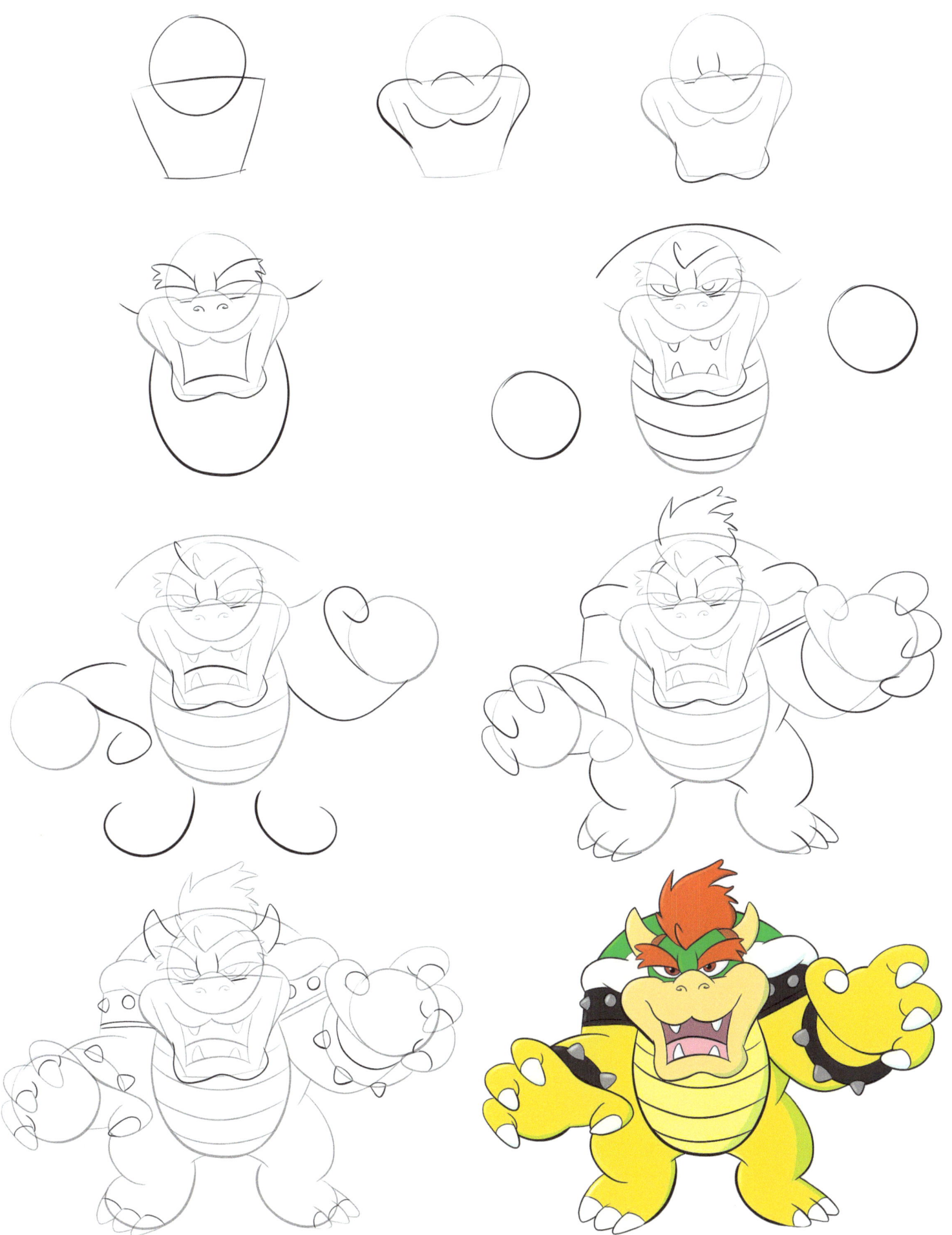

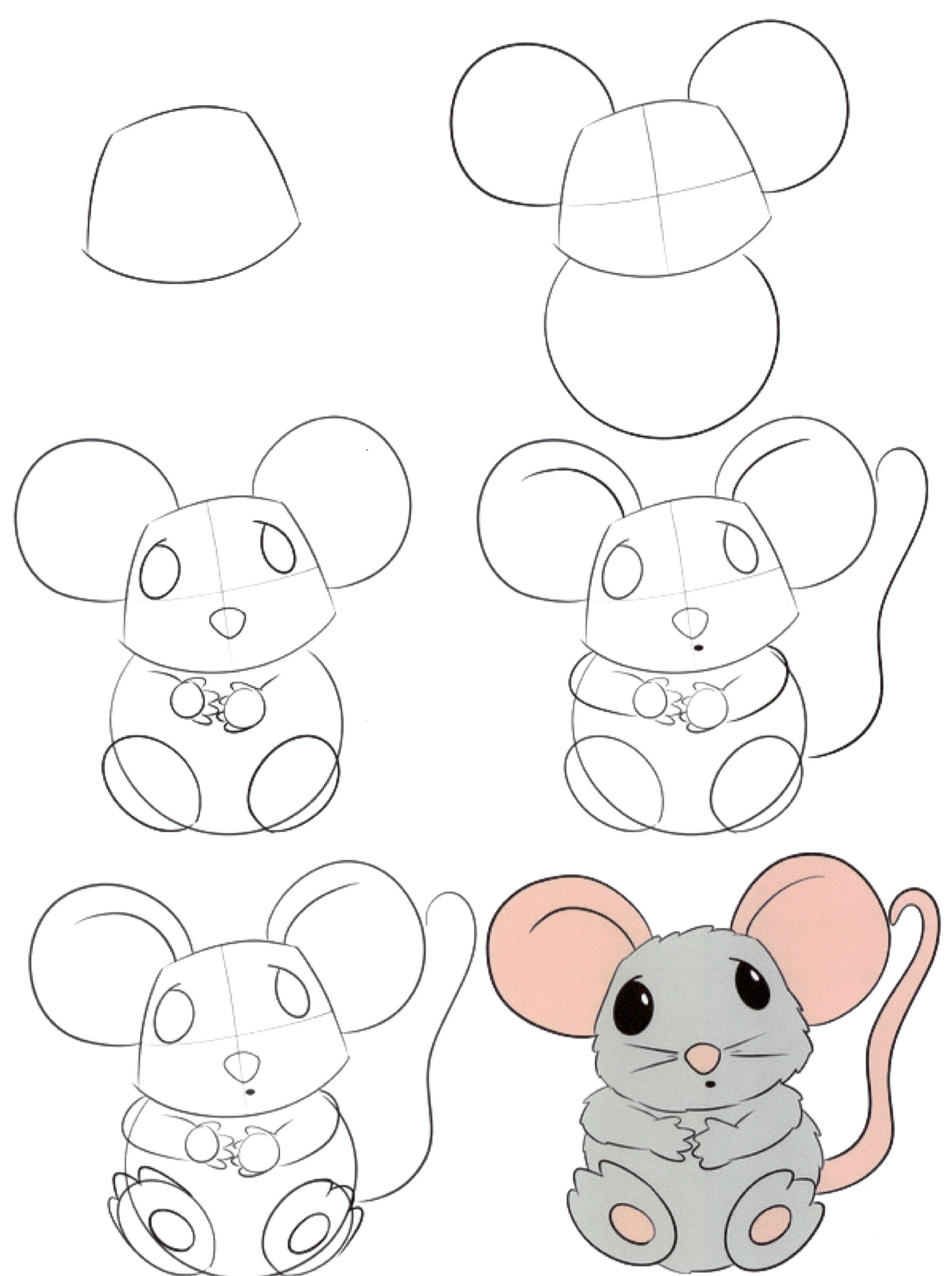

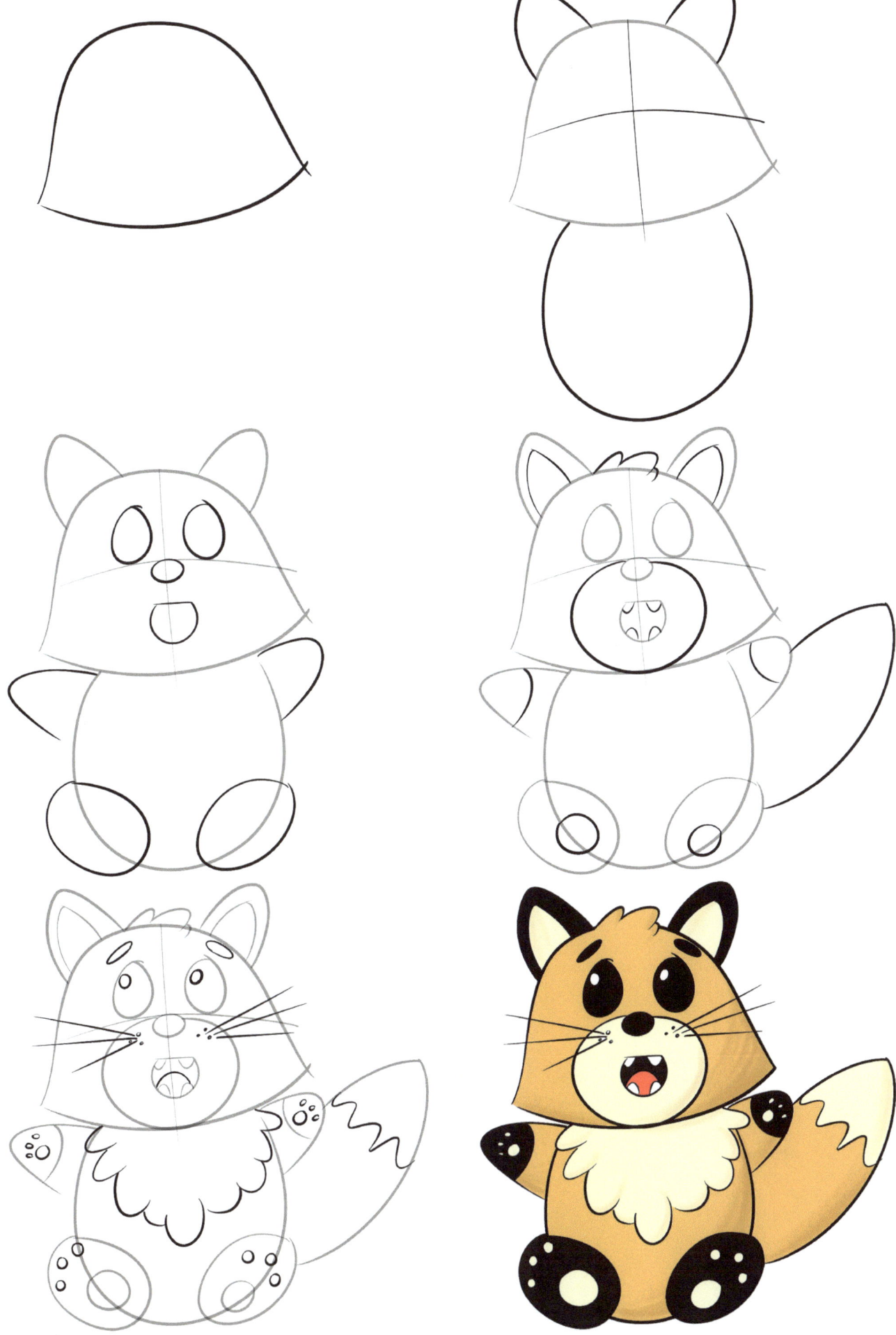

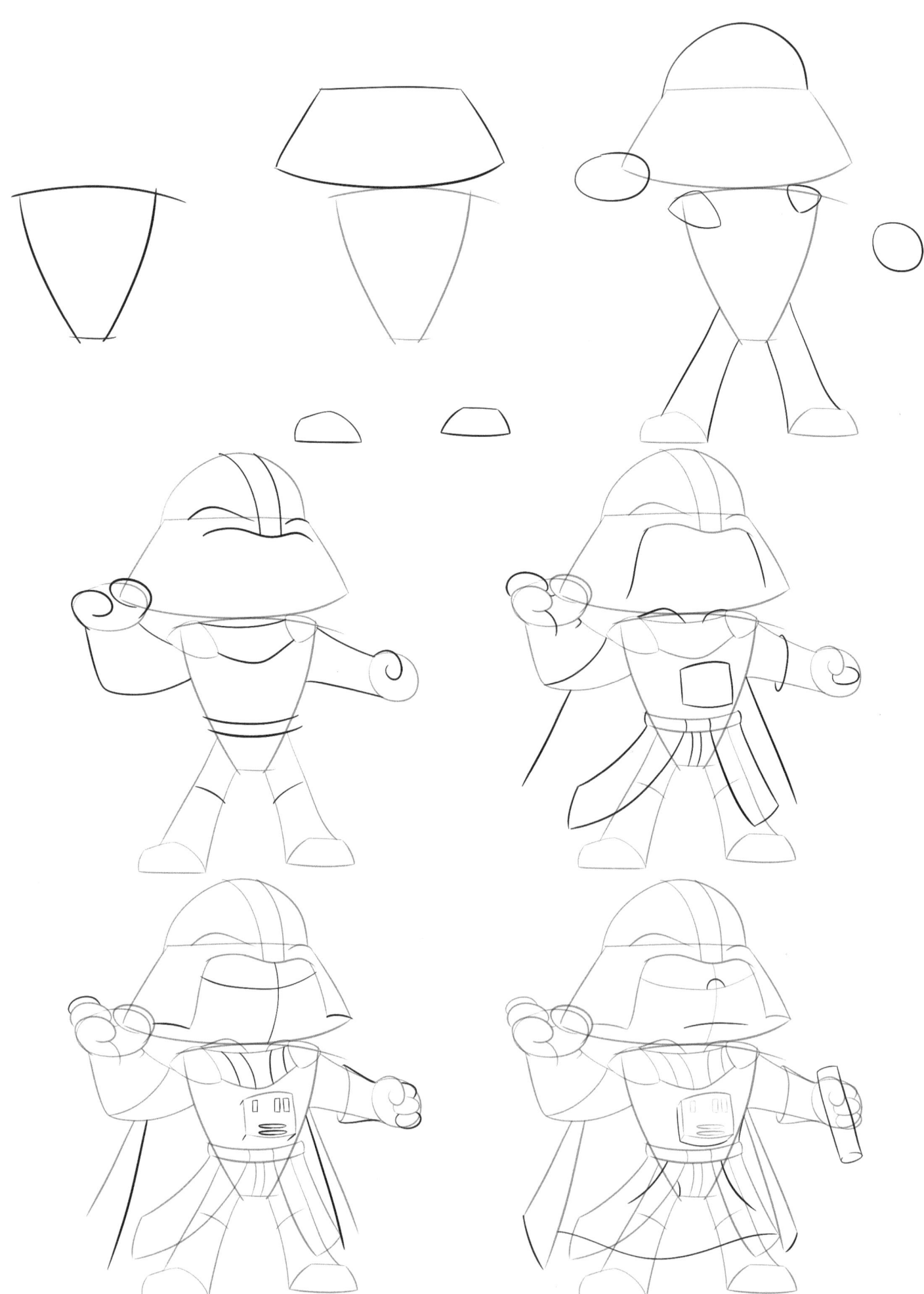

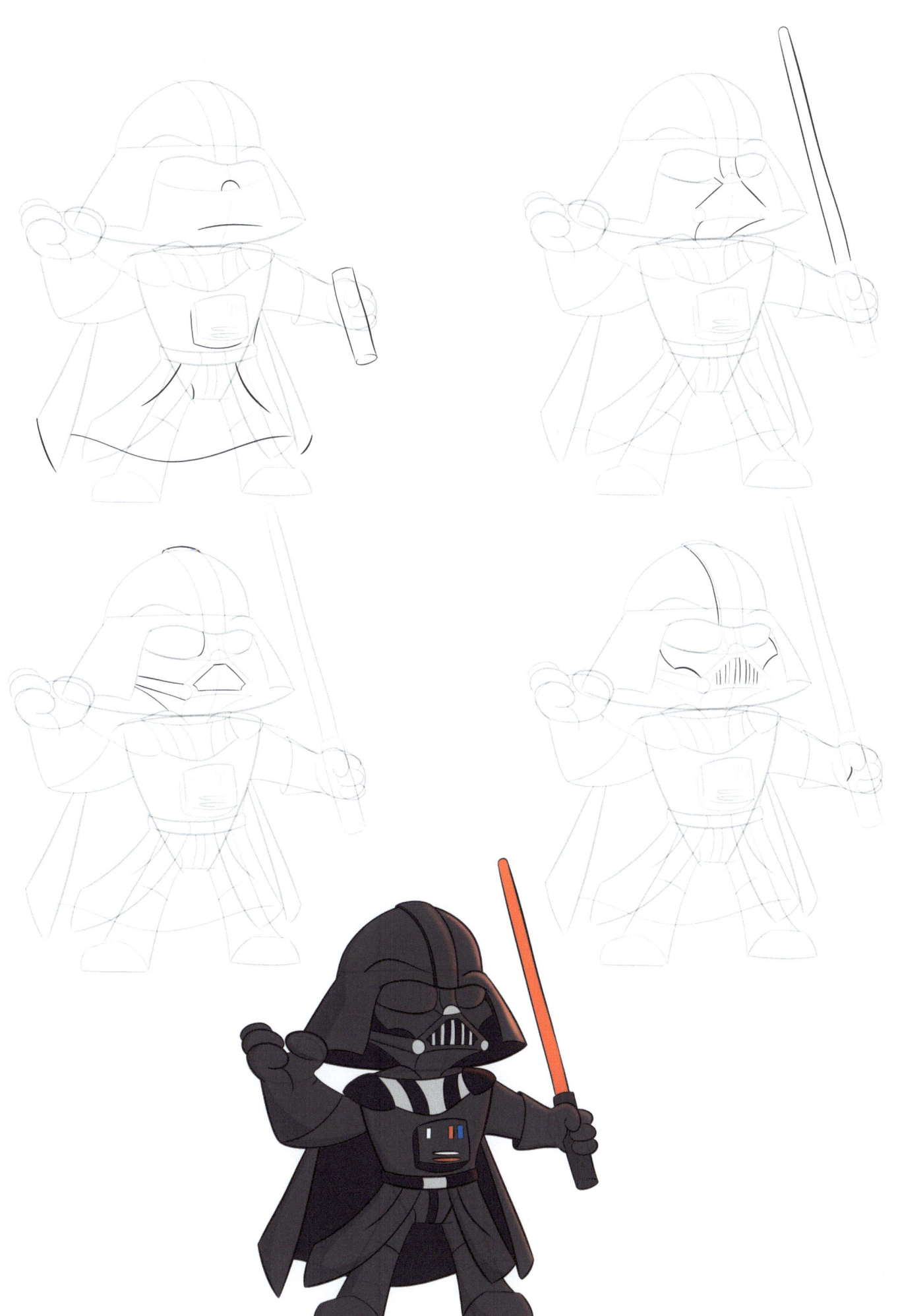

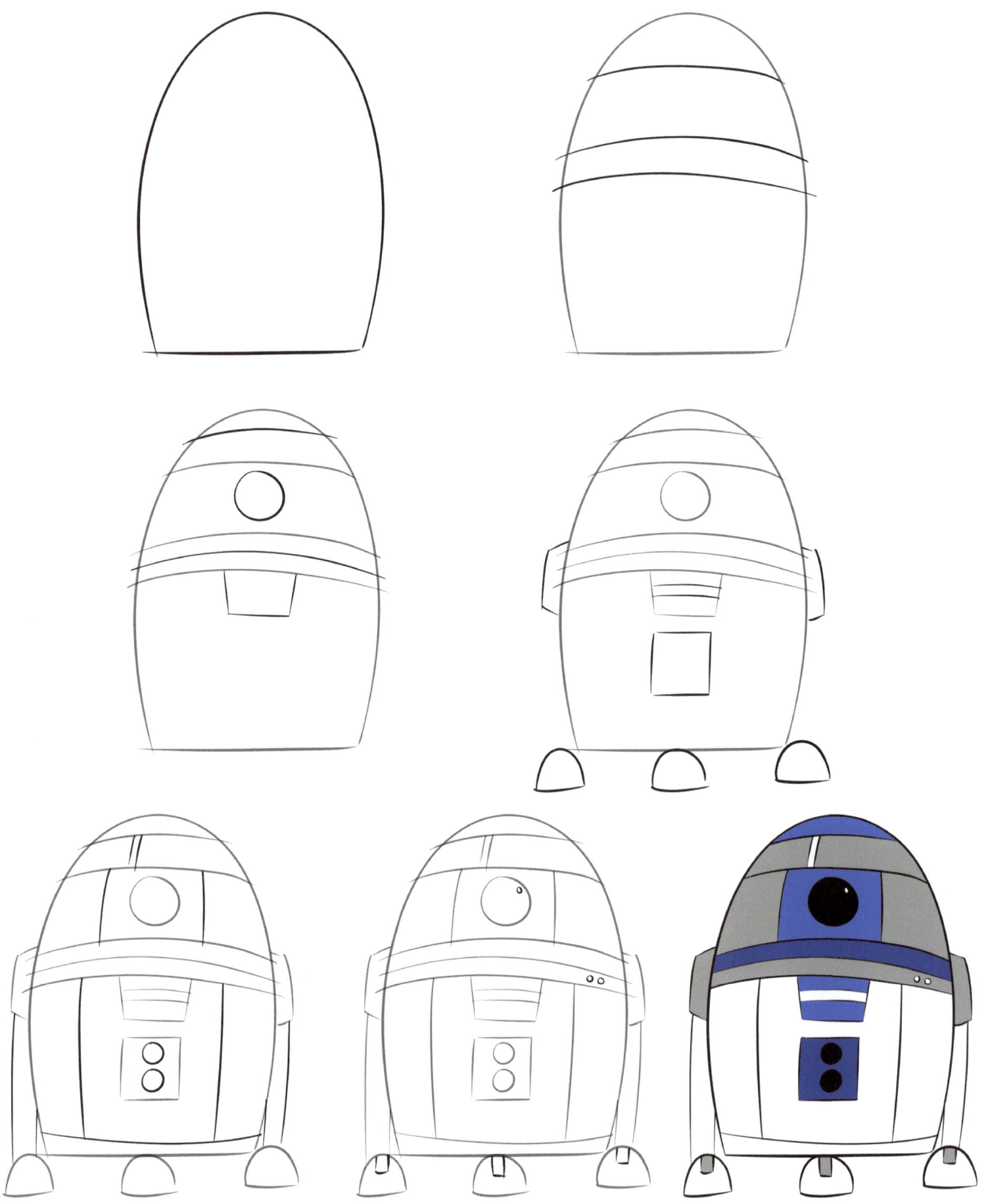

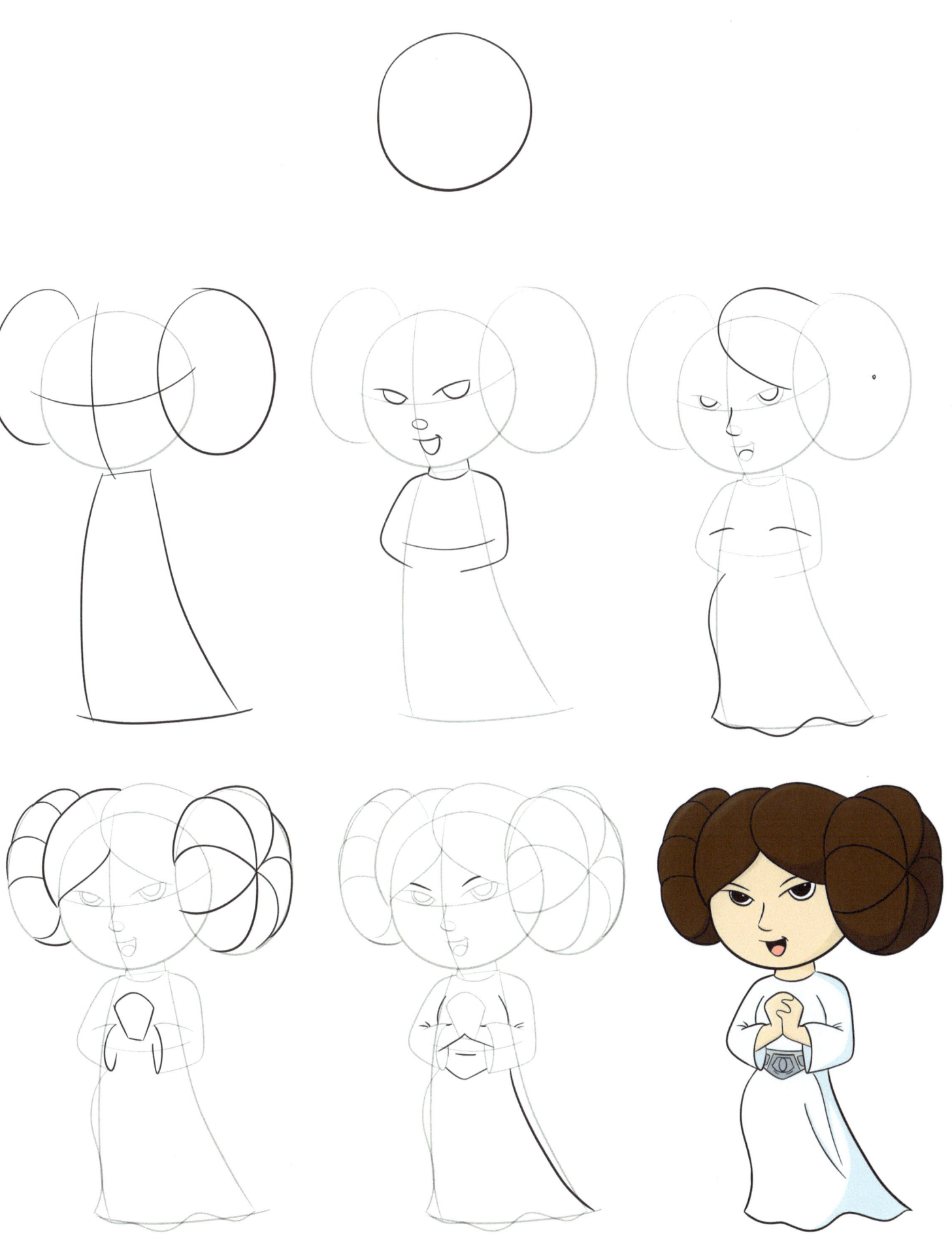

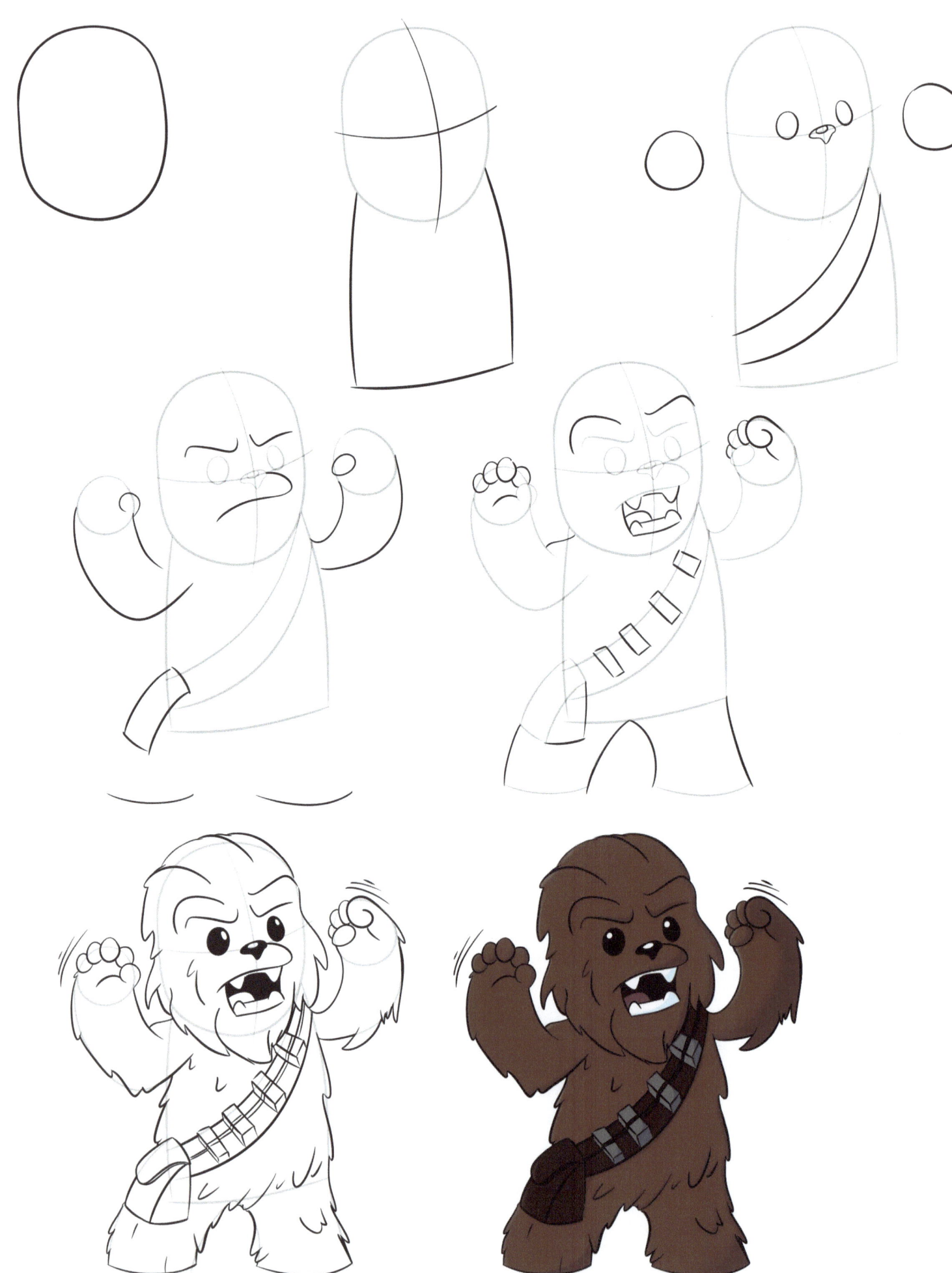

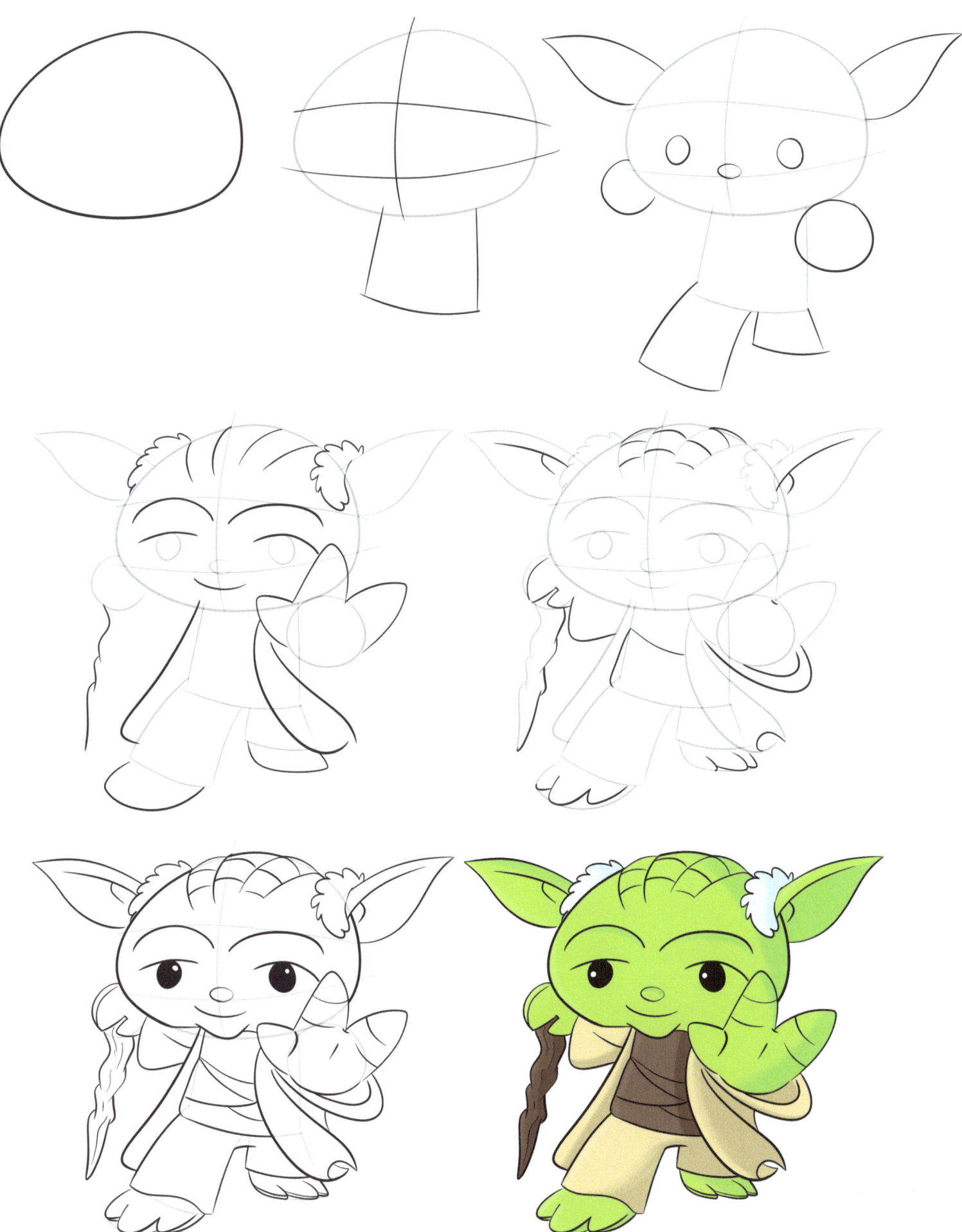

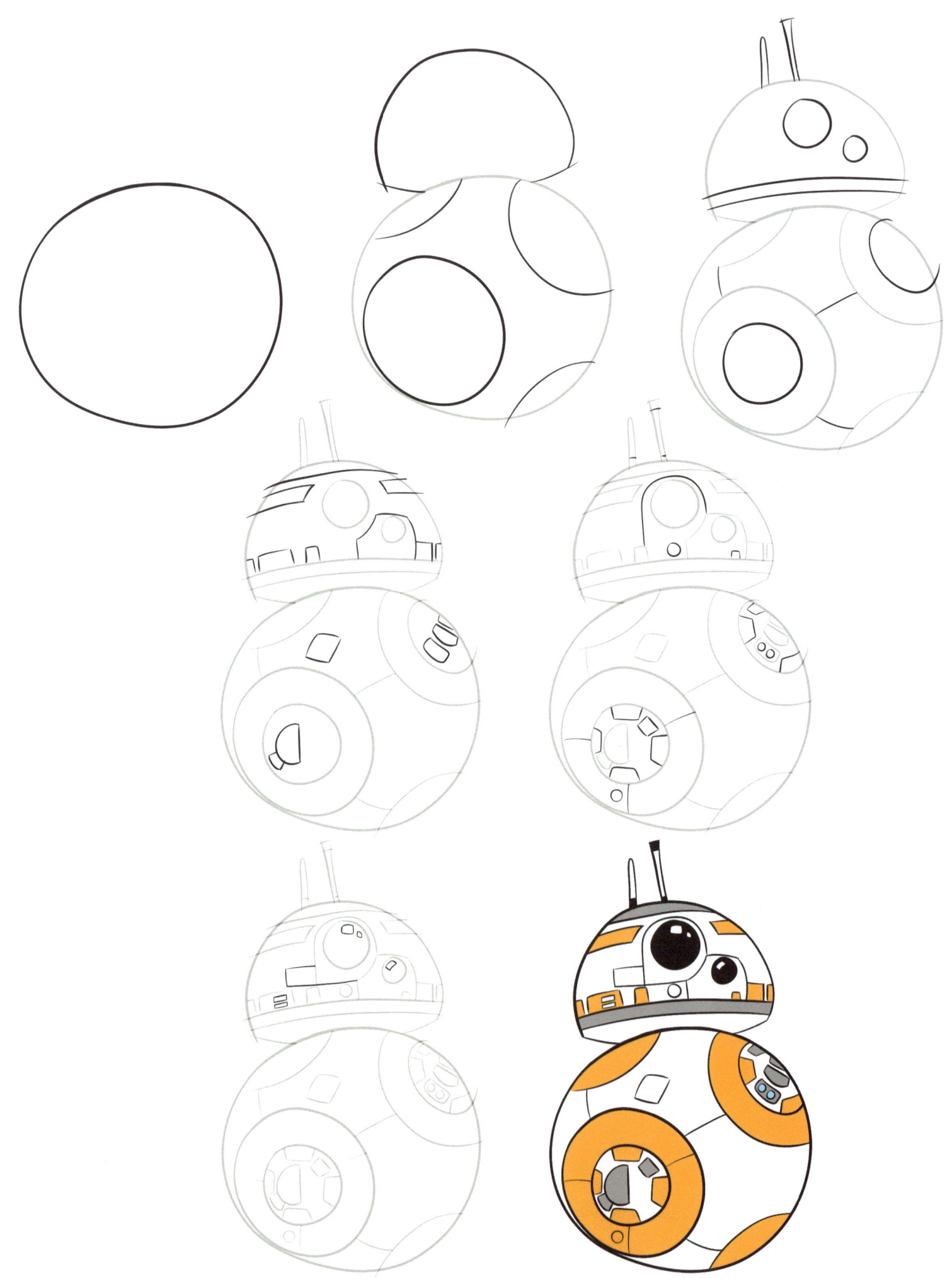

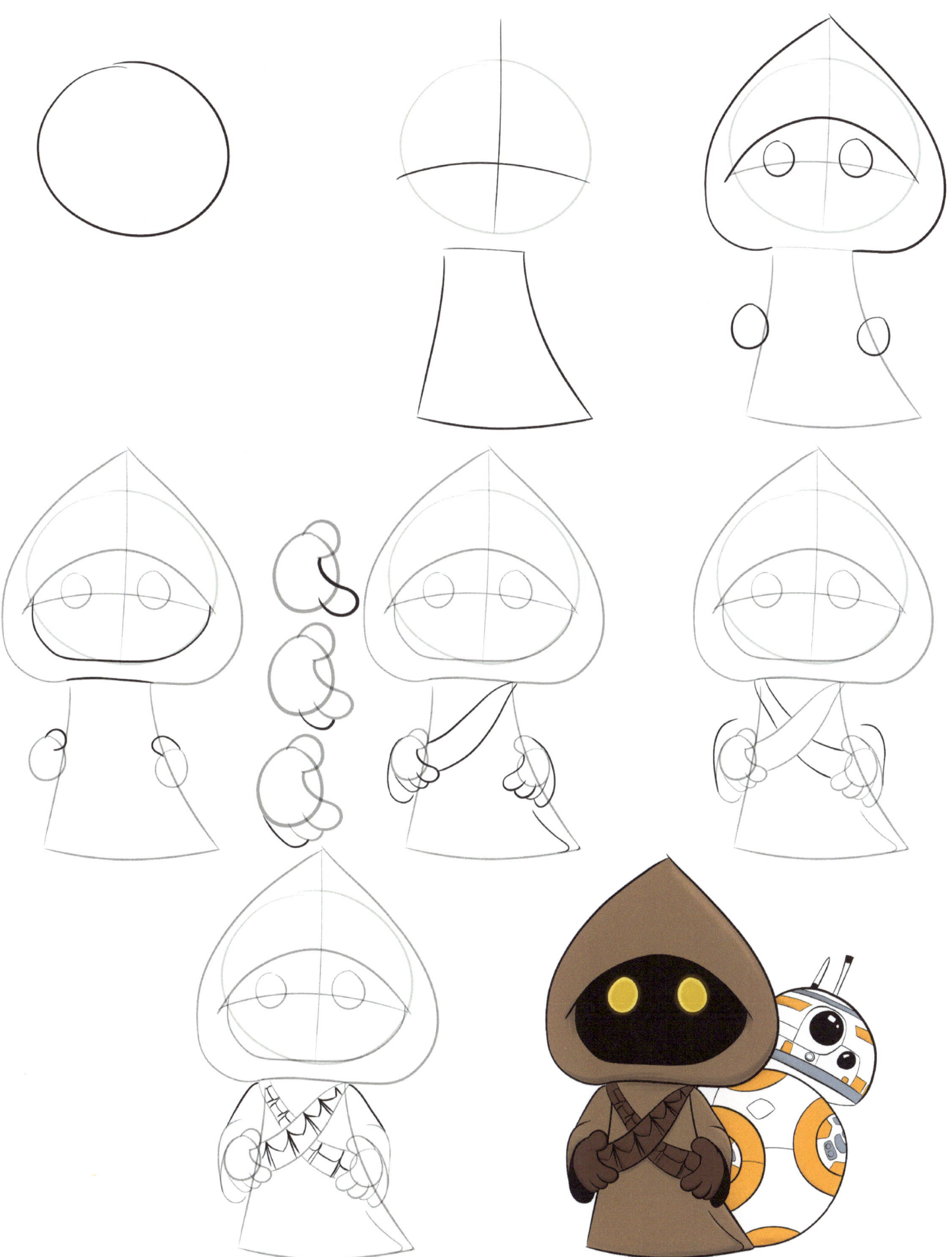

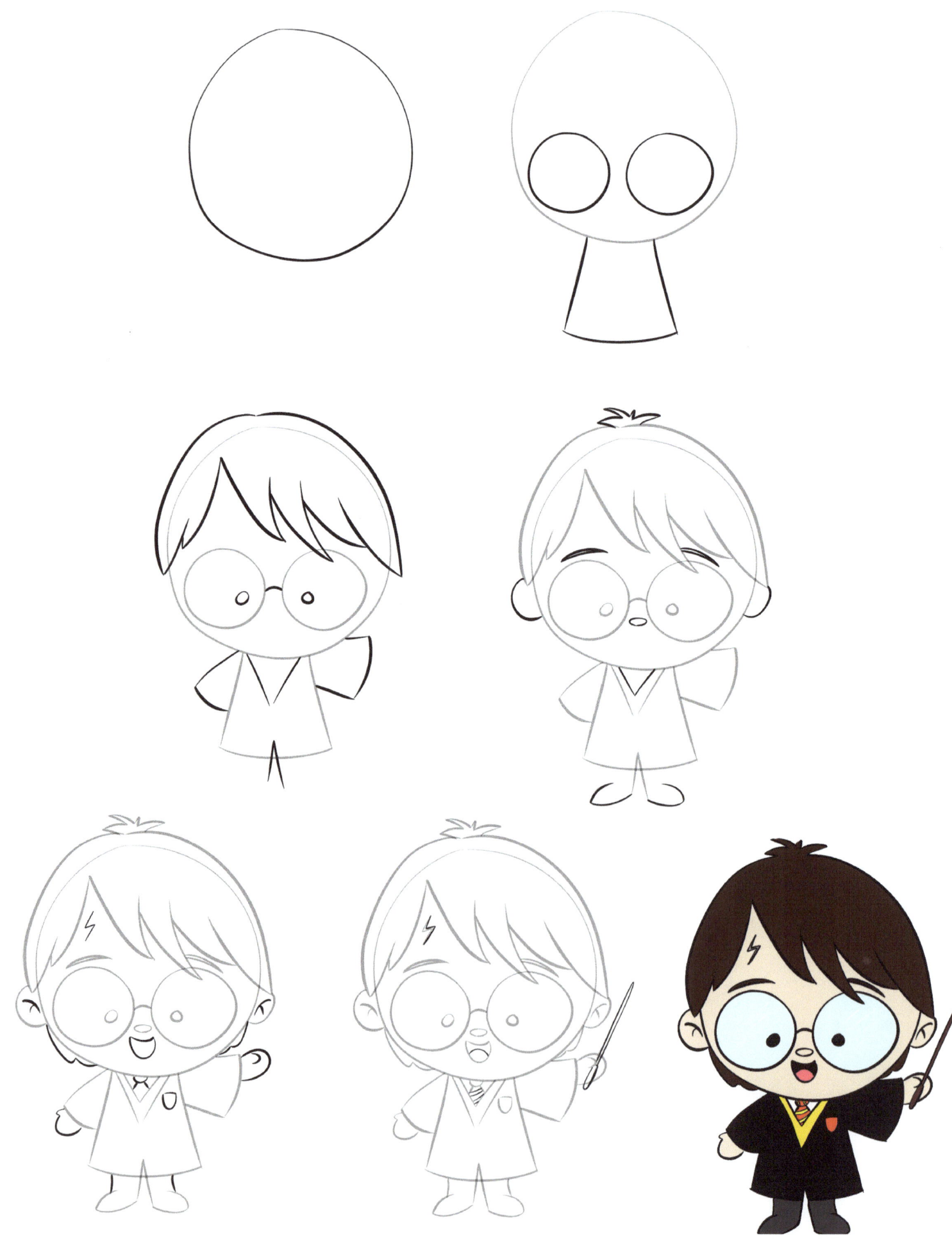

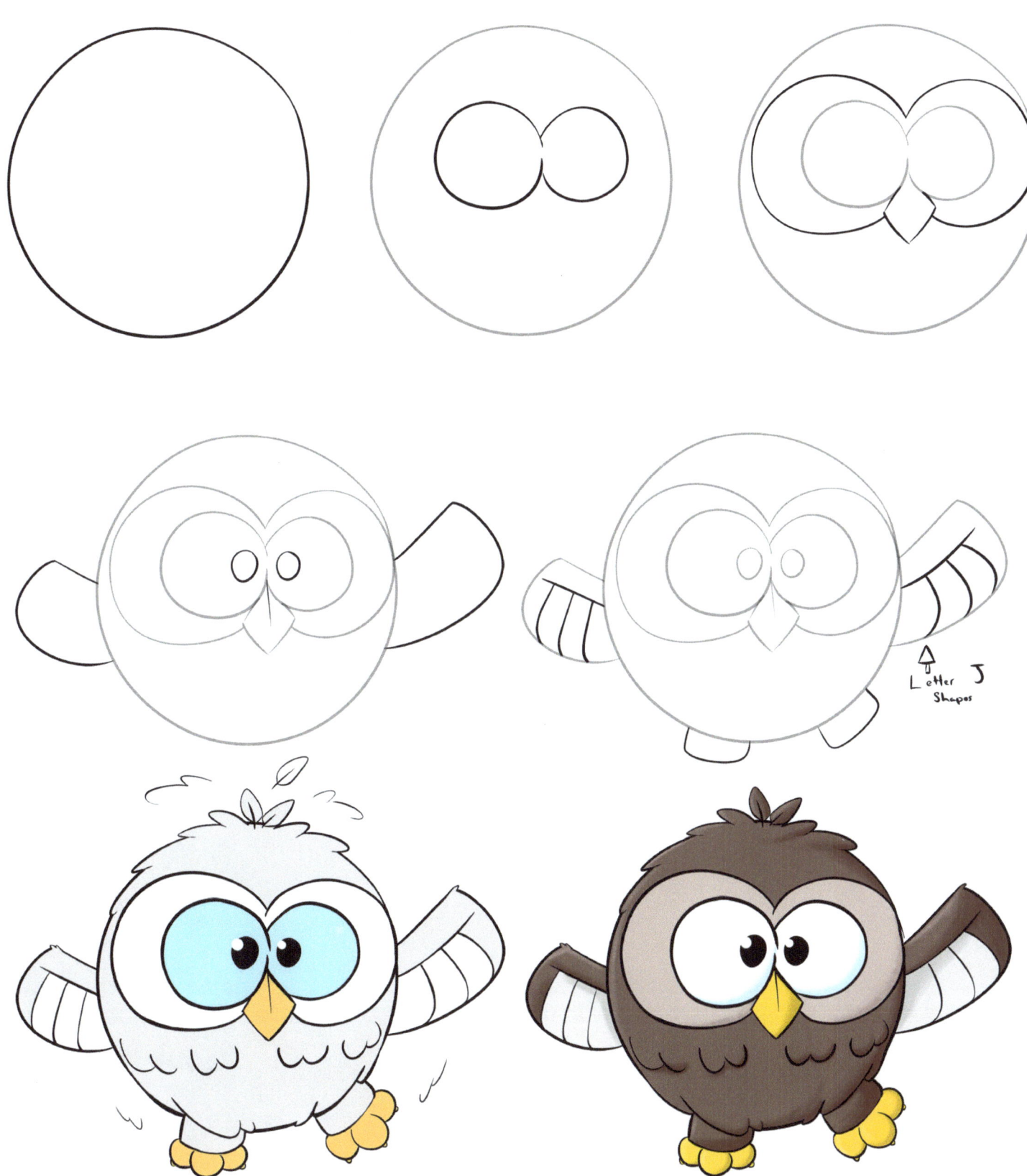

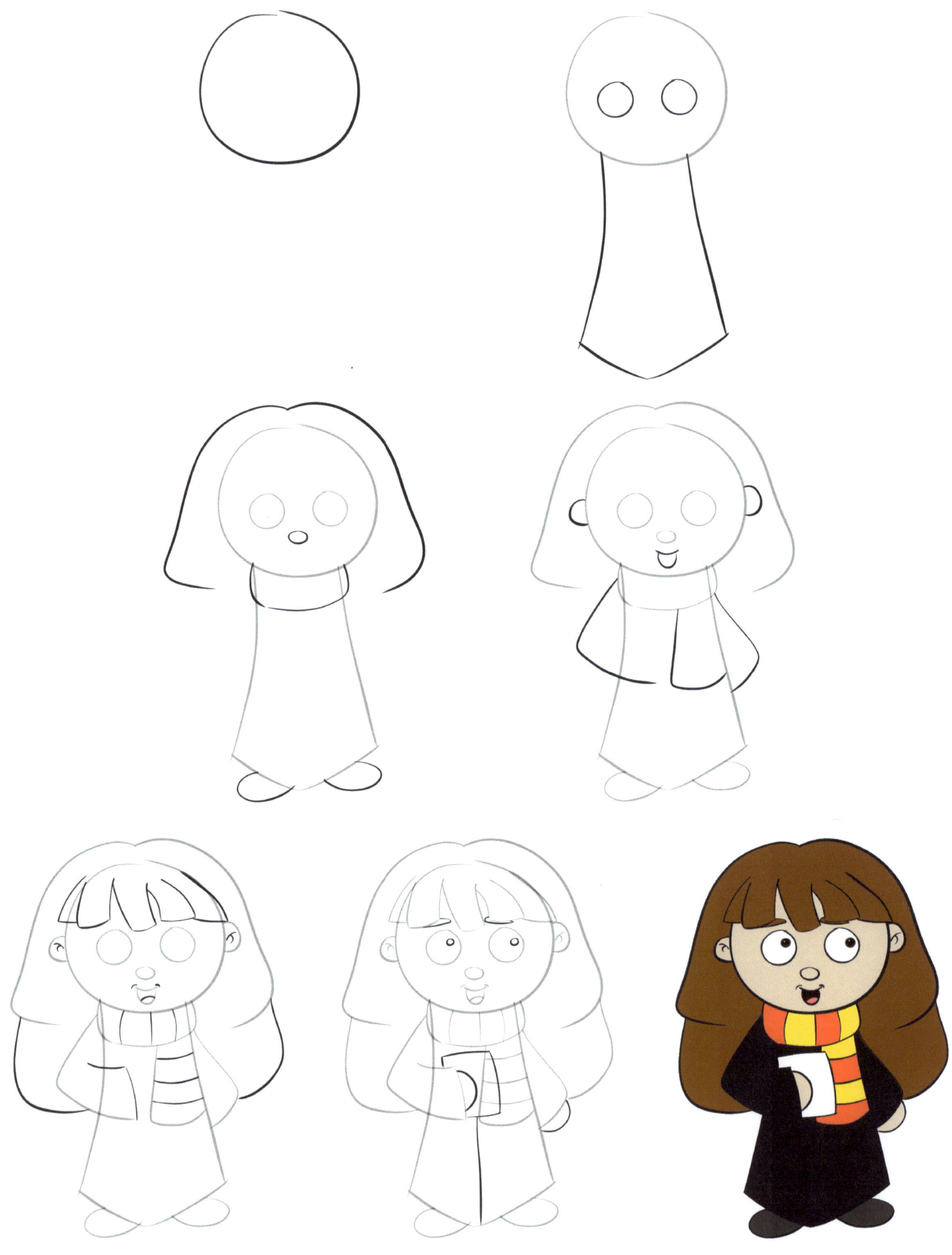

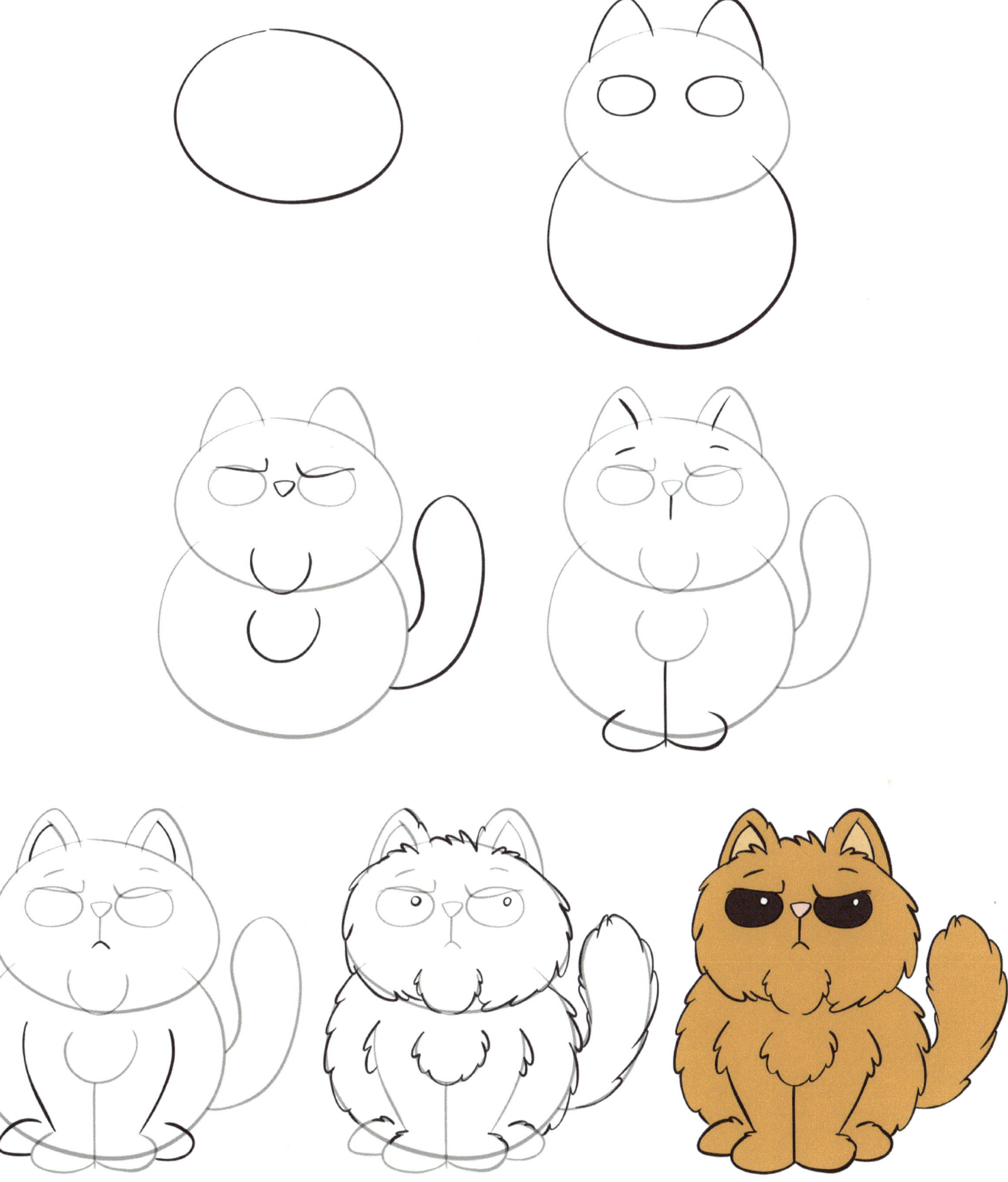

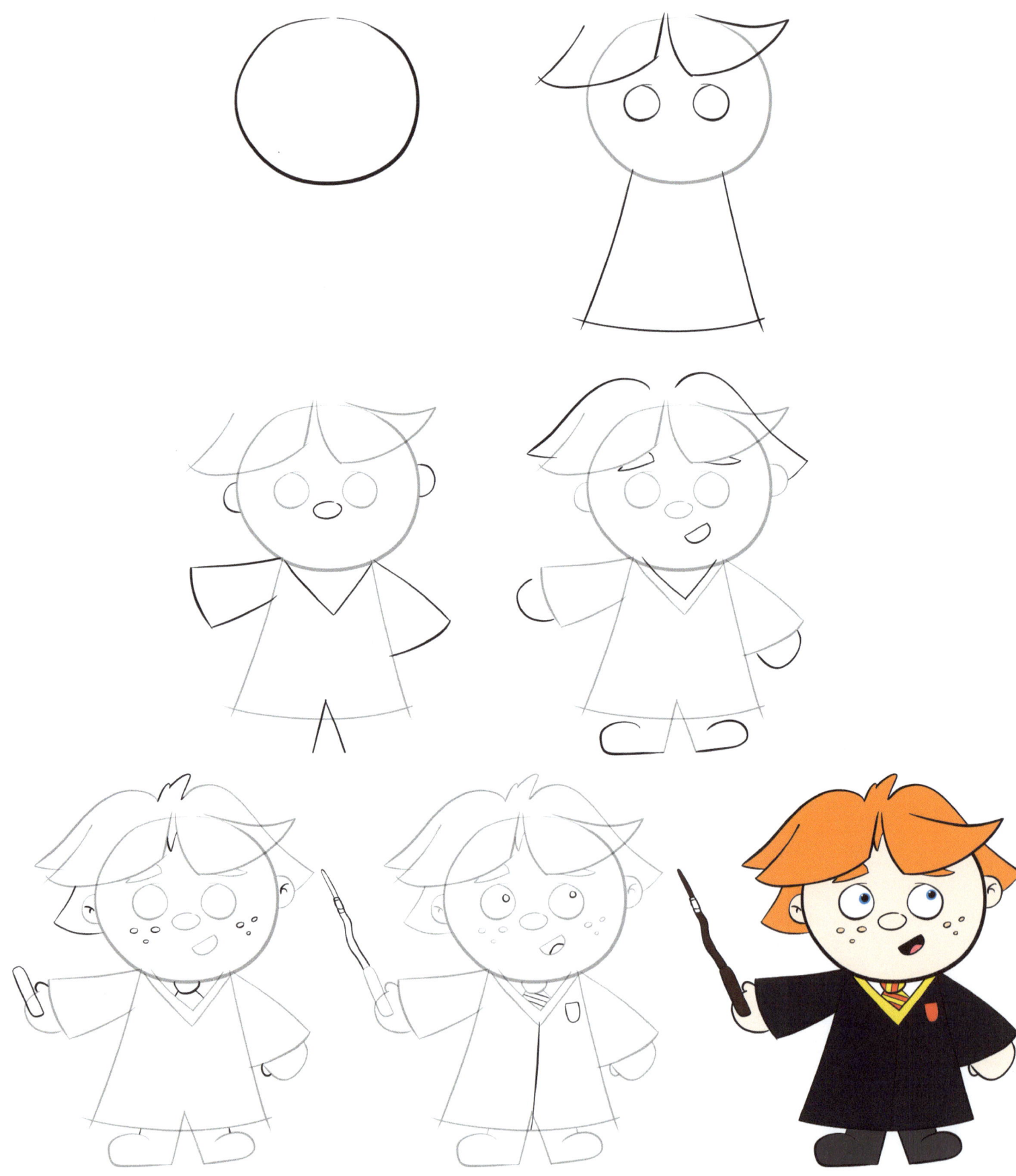

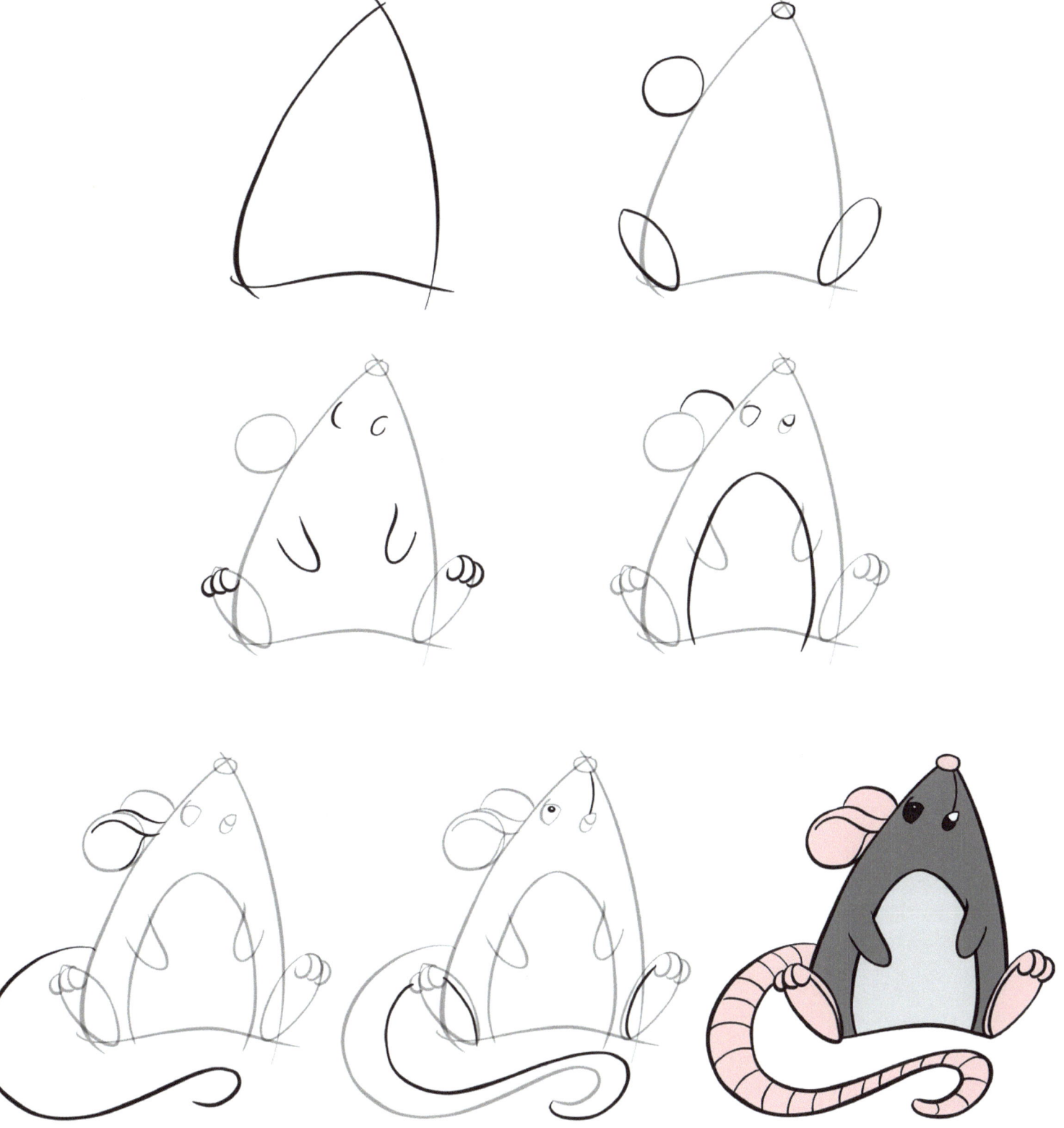

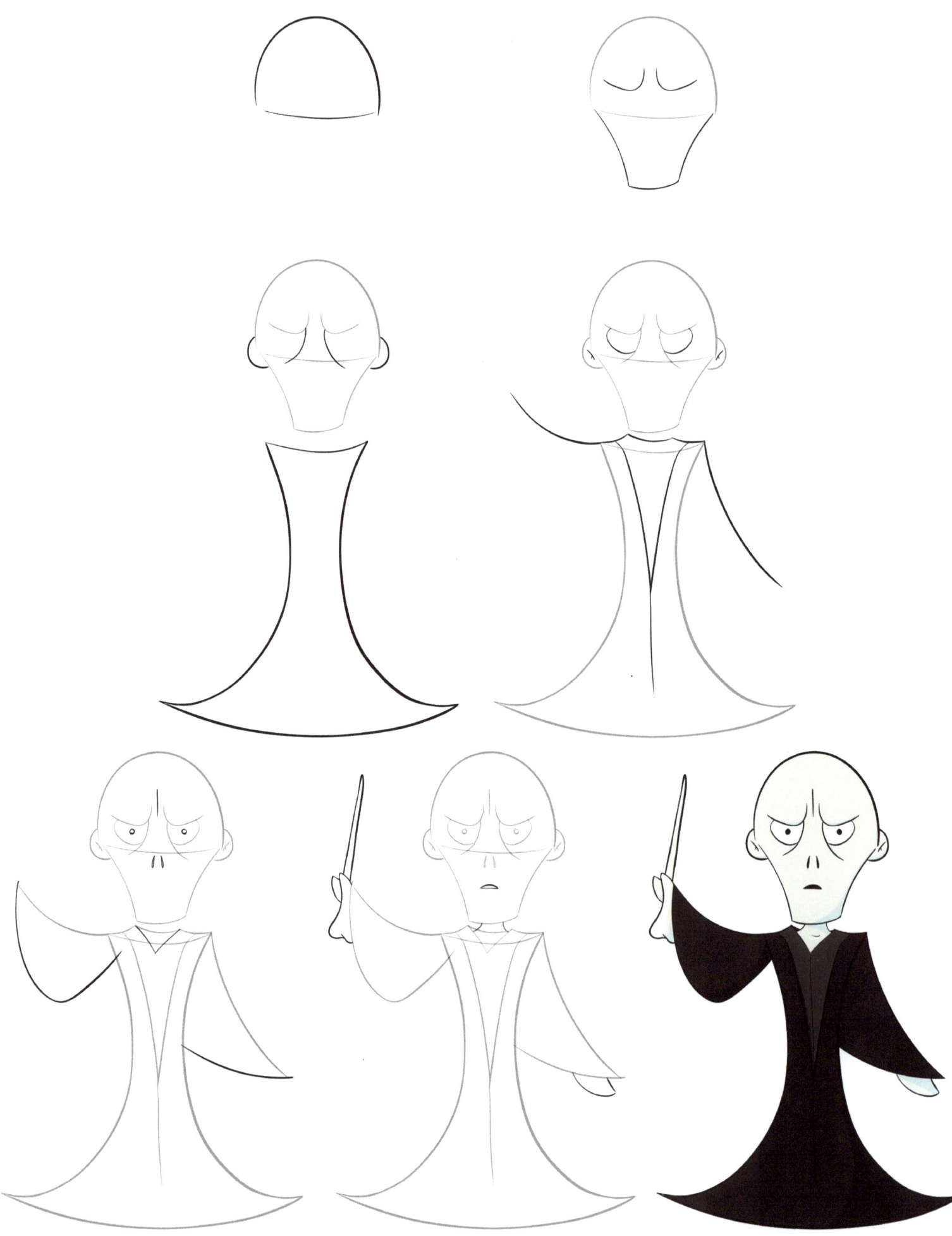

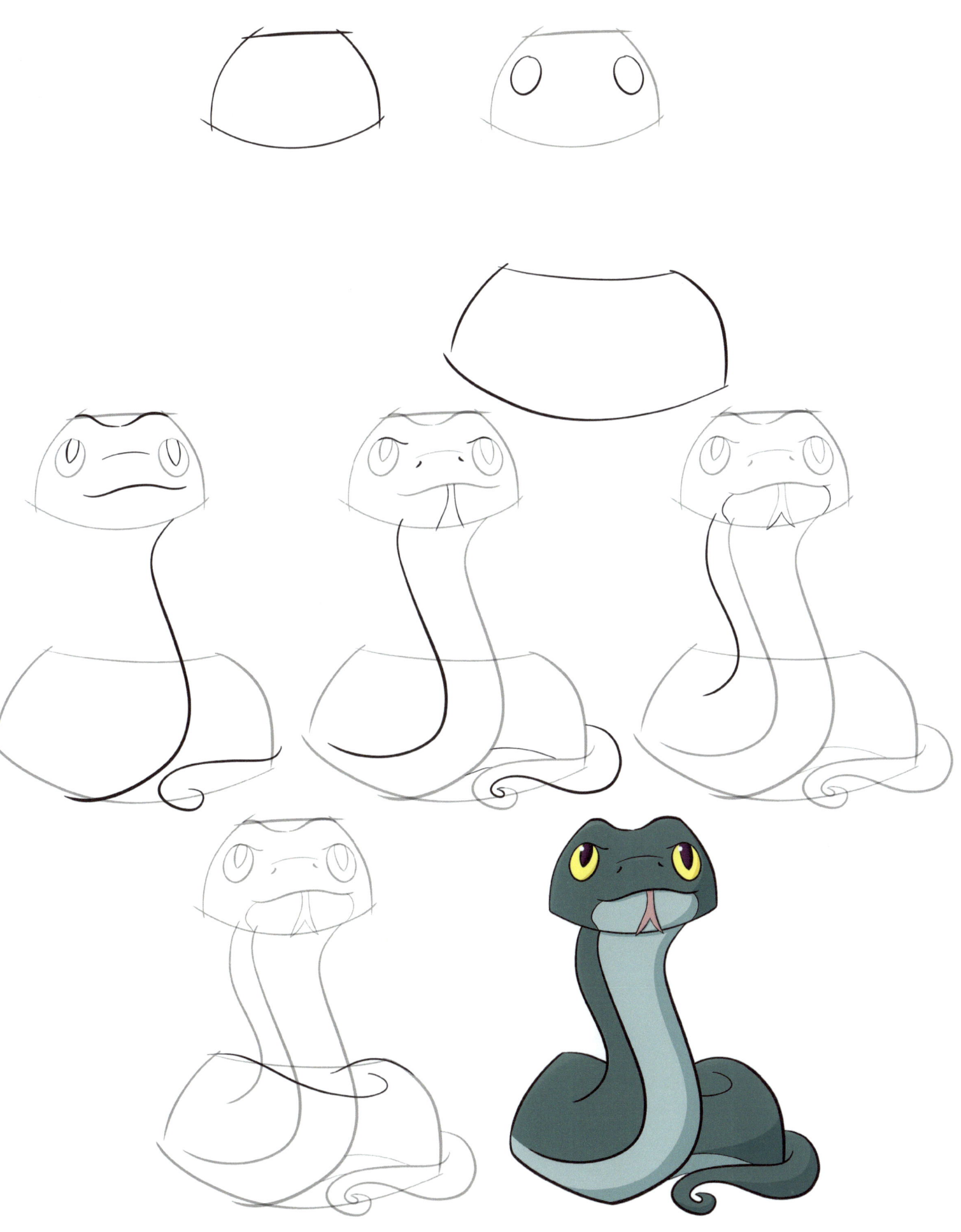

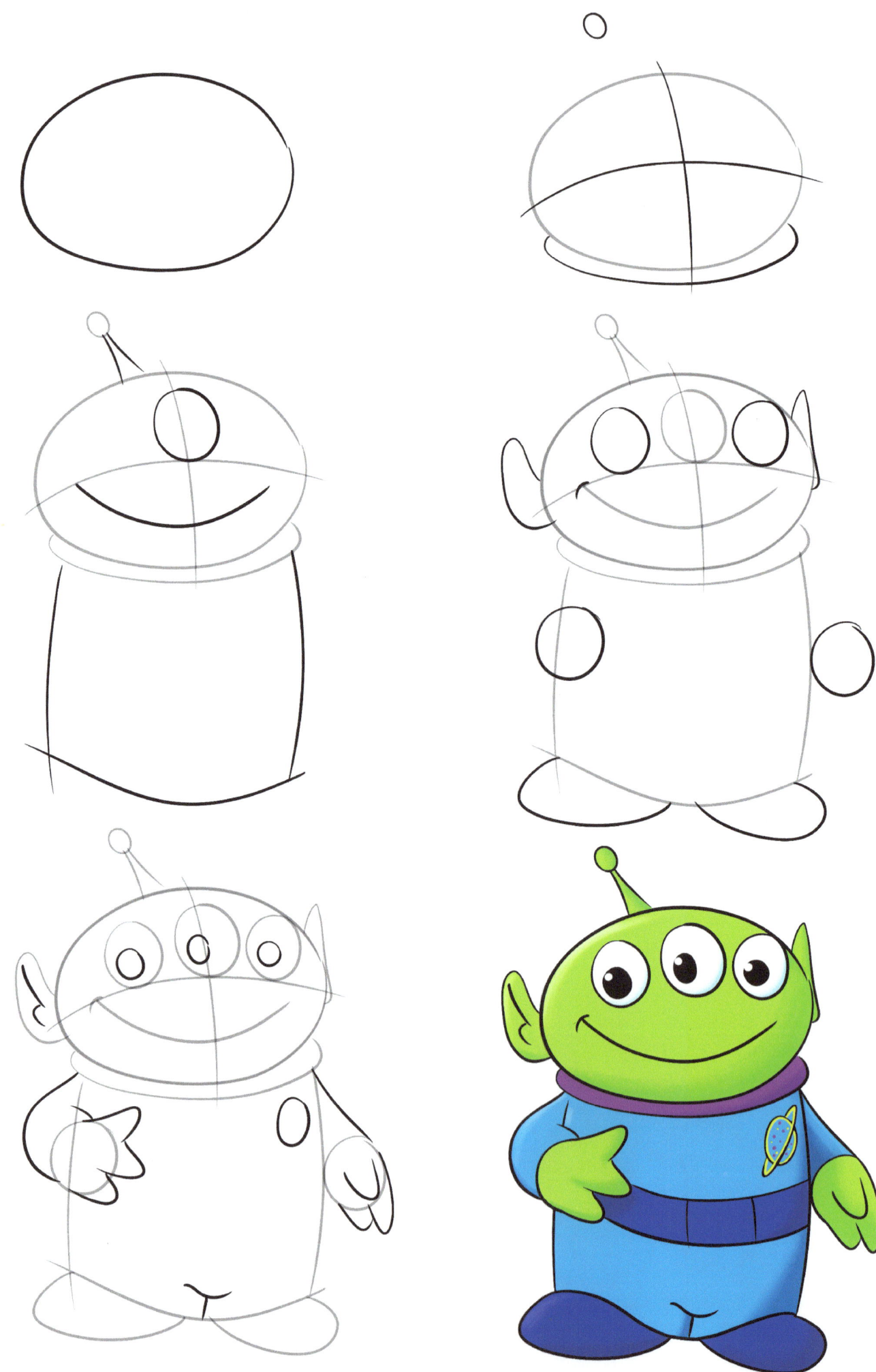

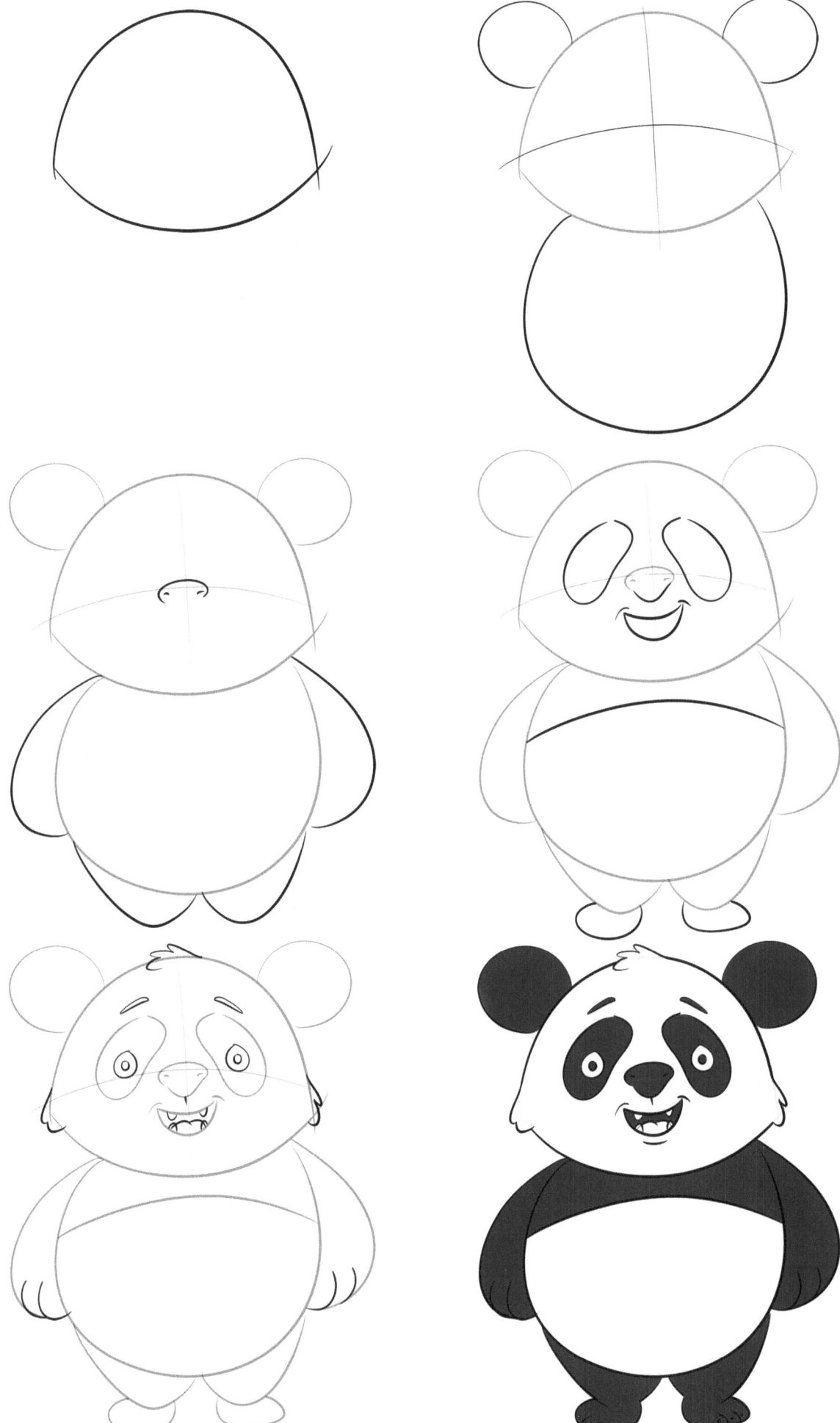

Simple Expressions with Eyebrows and Mouth

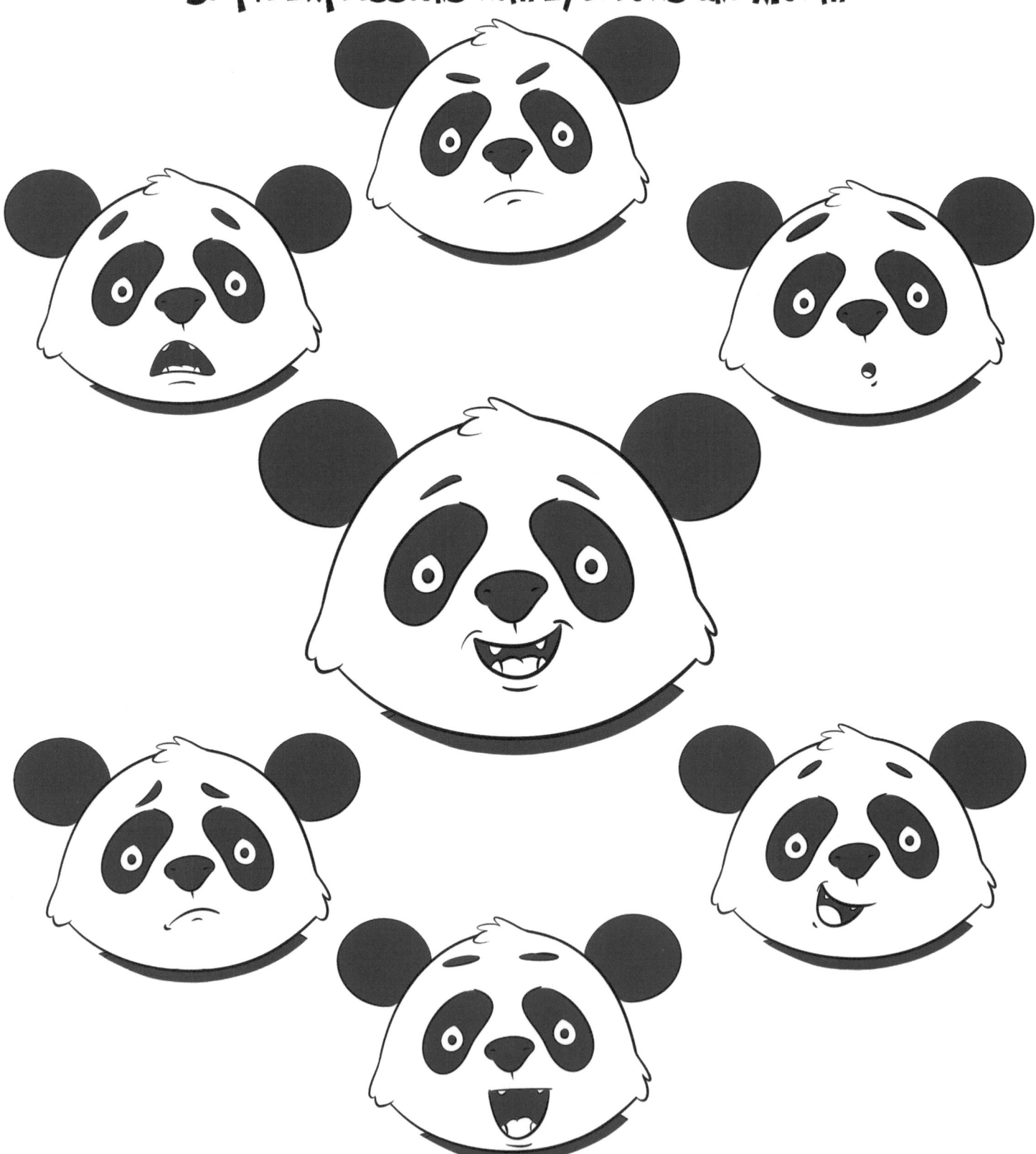

By using eyebrow and mouth shapes alone you can change the expressions and mood of the character. Next I will take this further by using the eye forms and cheeks to help increase expressions.

Push your Expressions with Brows and Cheeks

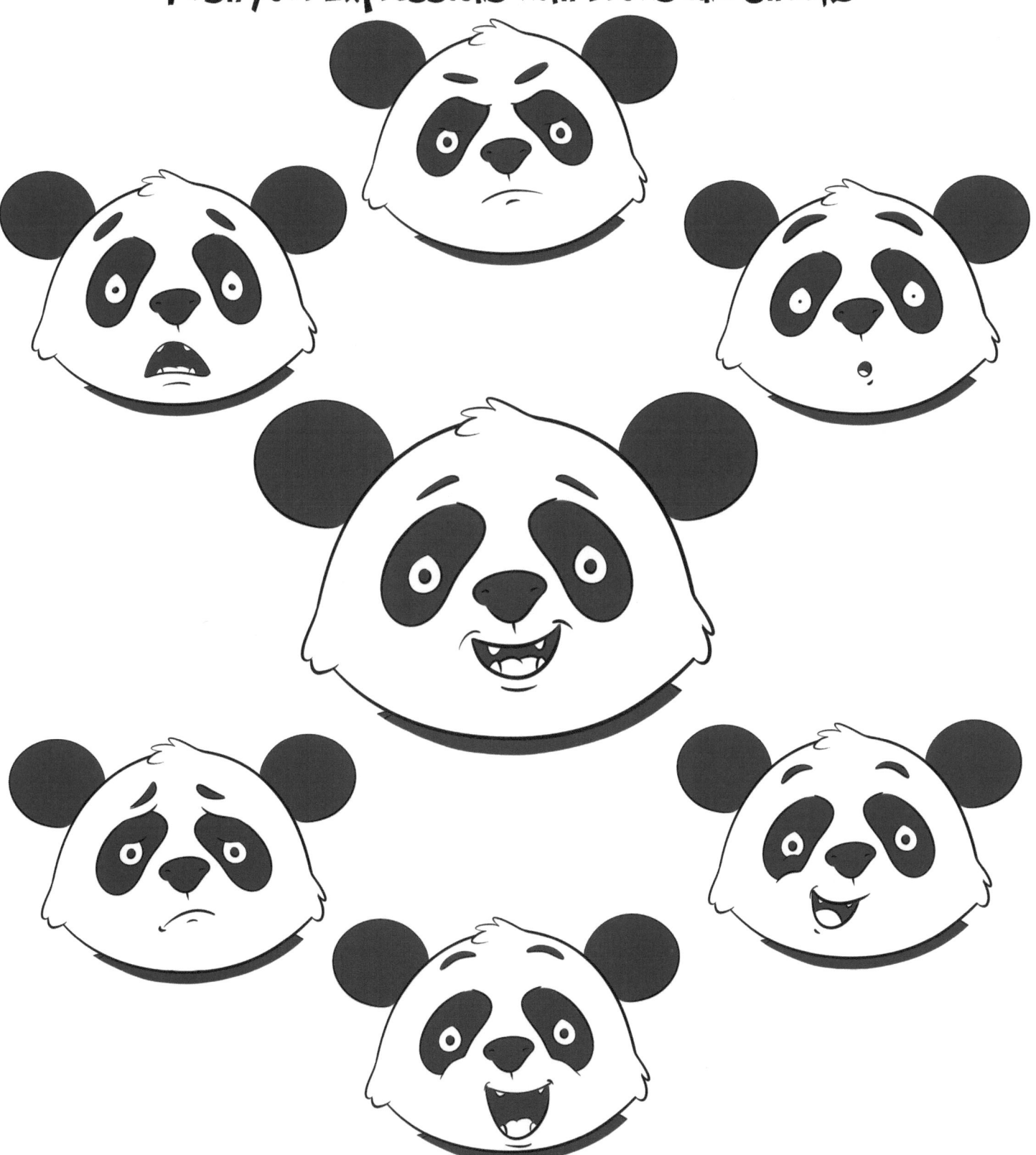

By using the brow and some cheeks you can push the expression further. By using the eye forms and brows in both size and shape, it helps to get the emotion across better than the original version. Using the cheek also pushes how happy the panda feels.

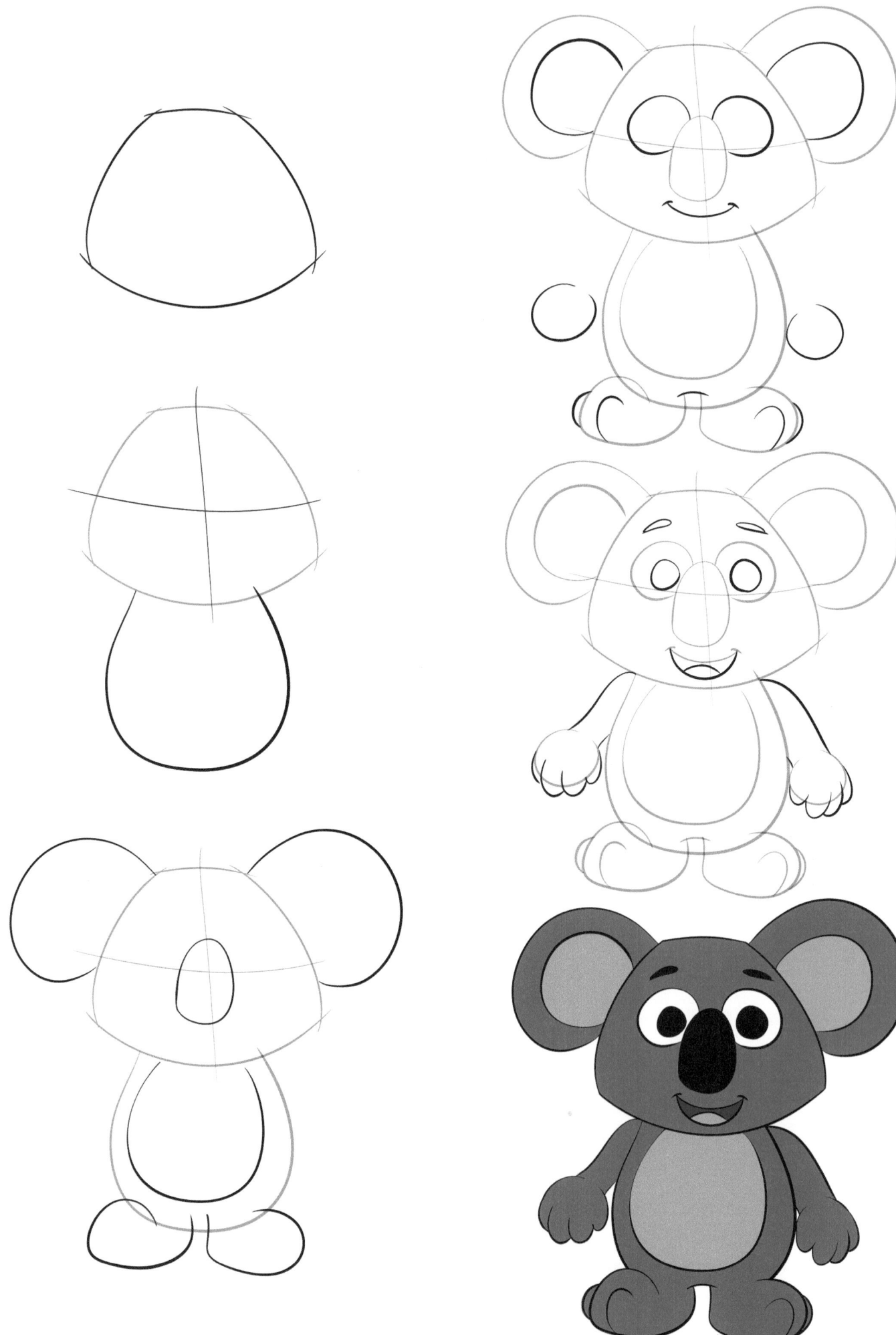

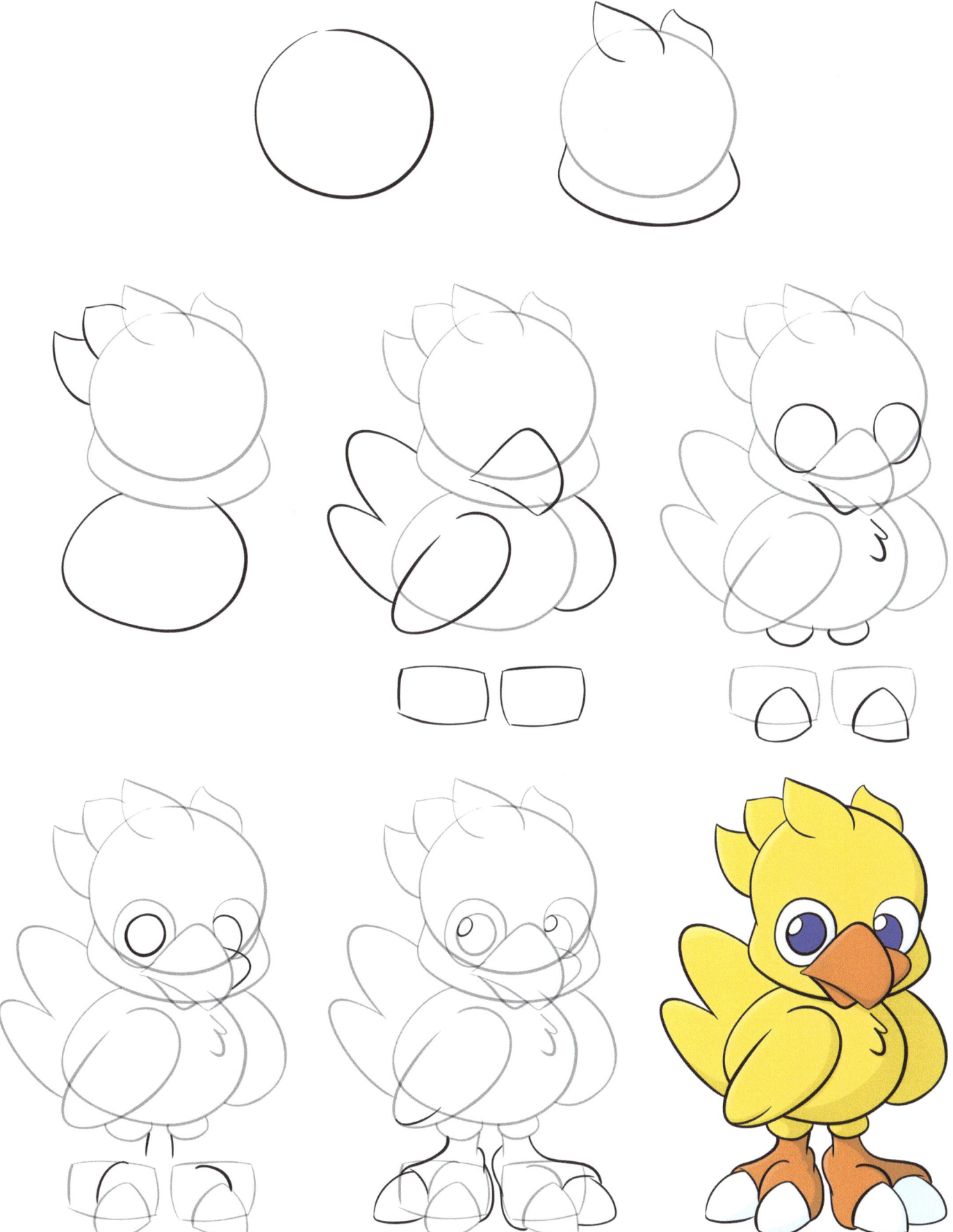

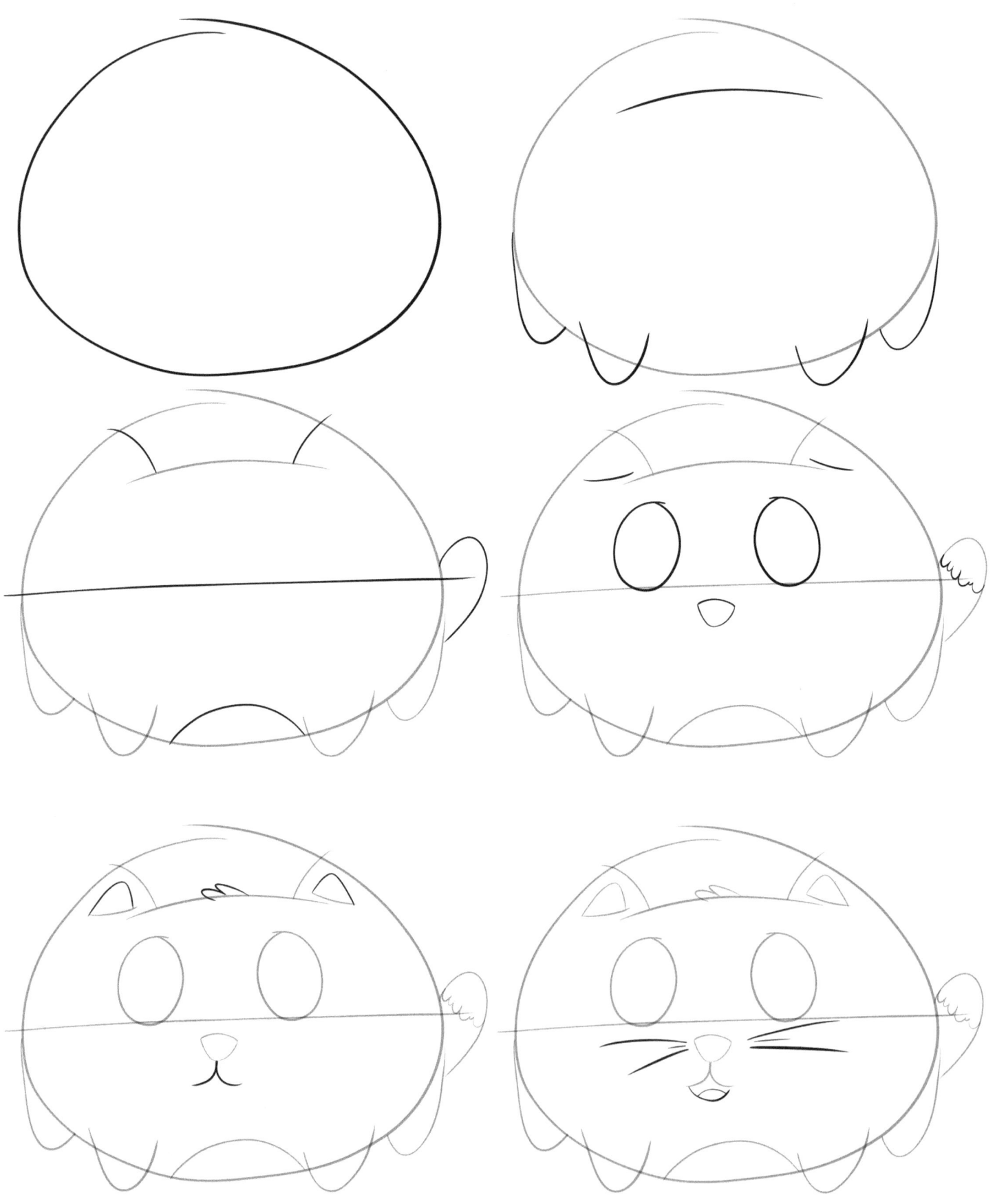

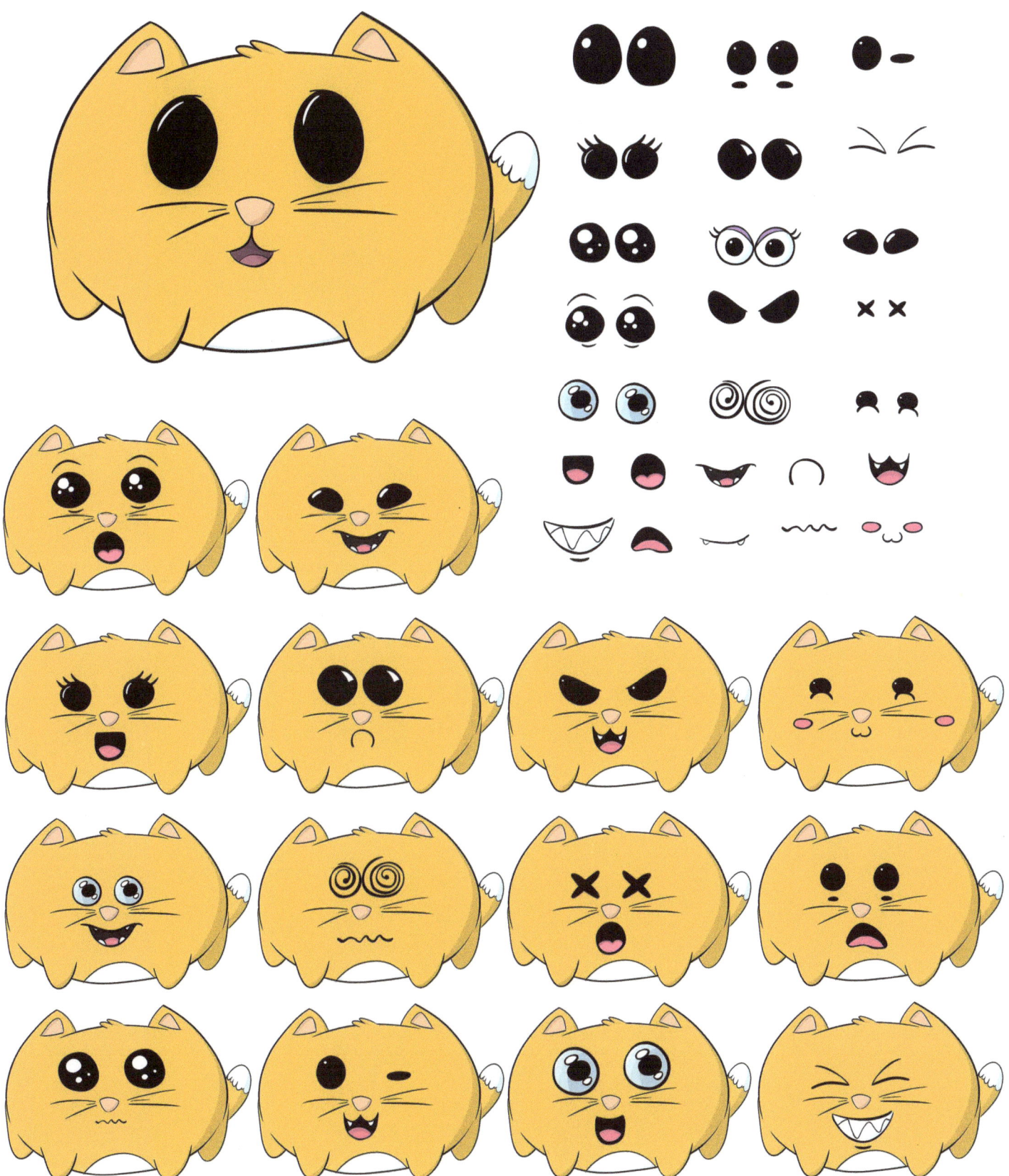

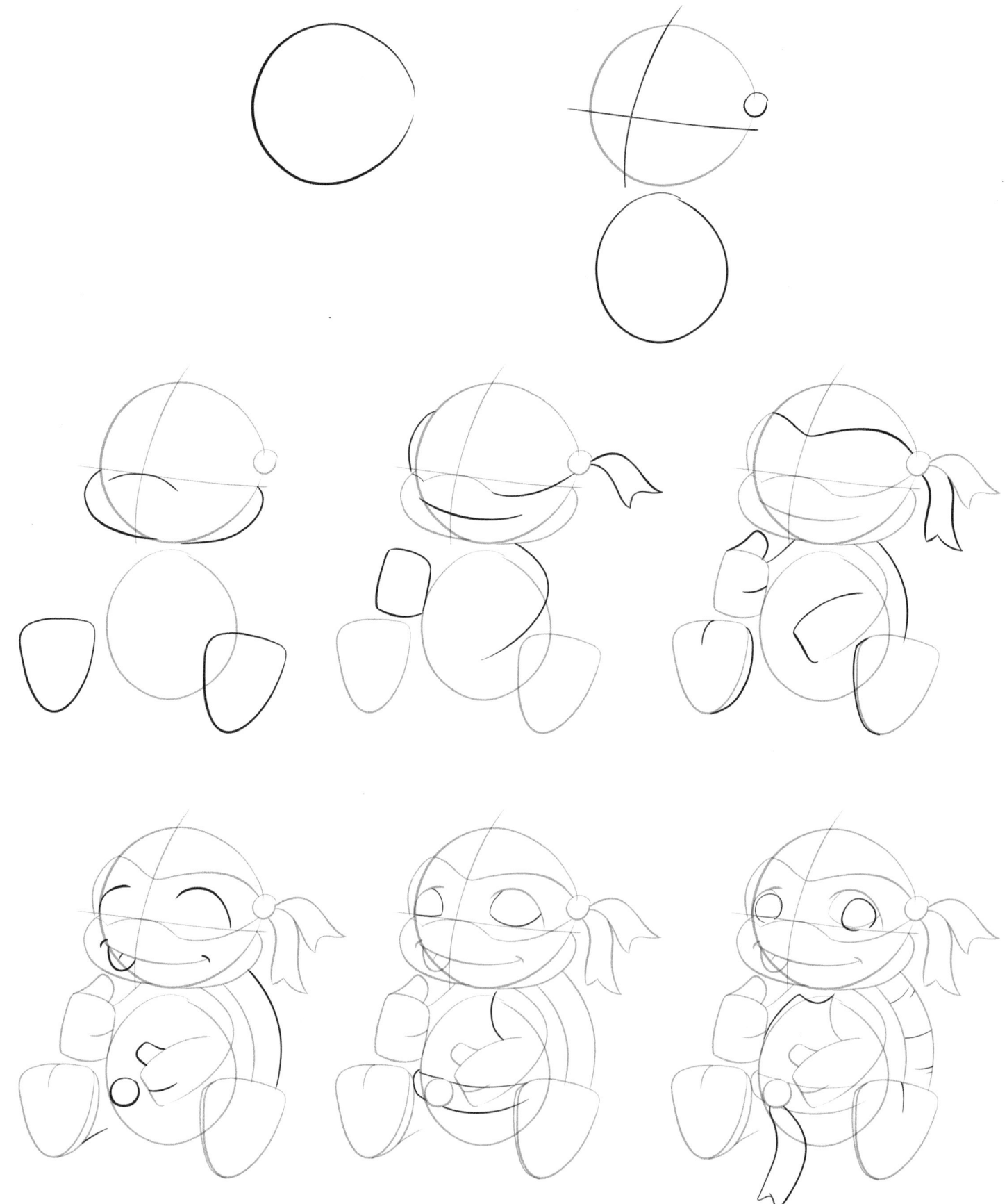

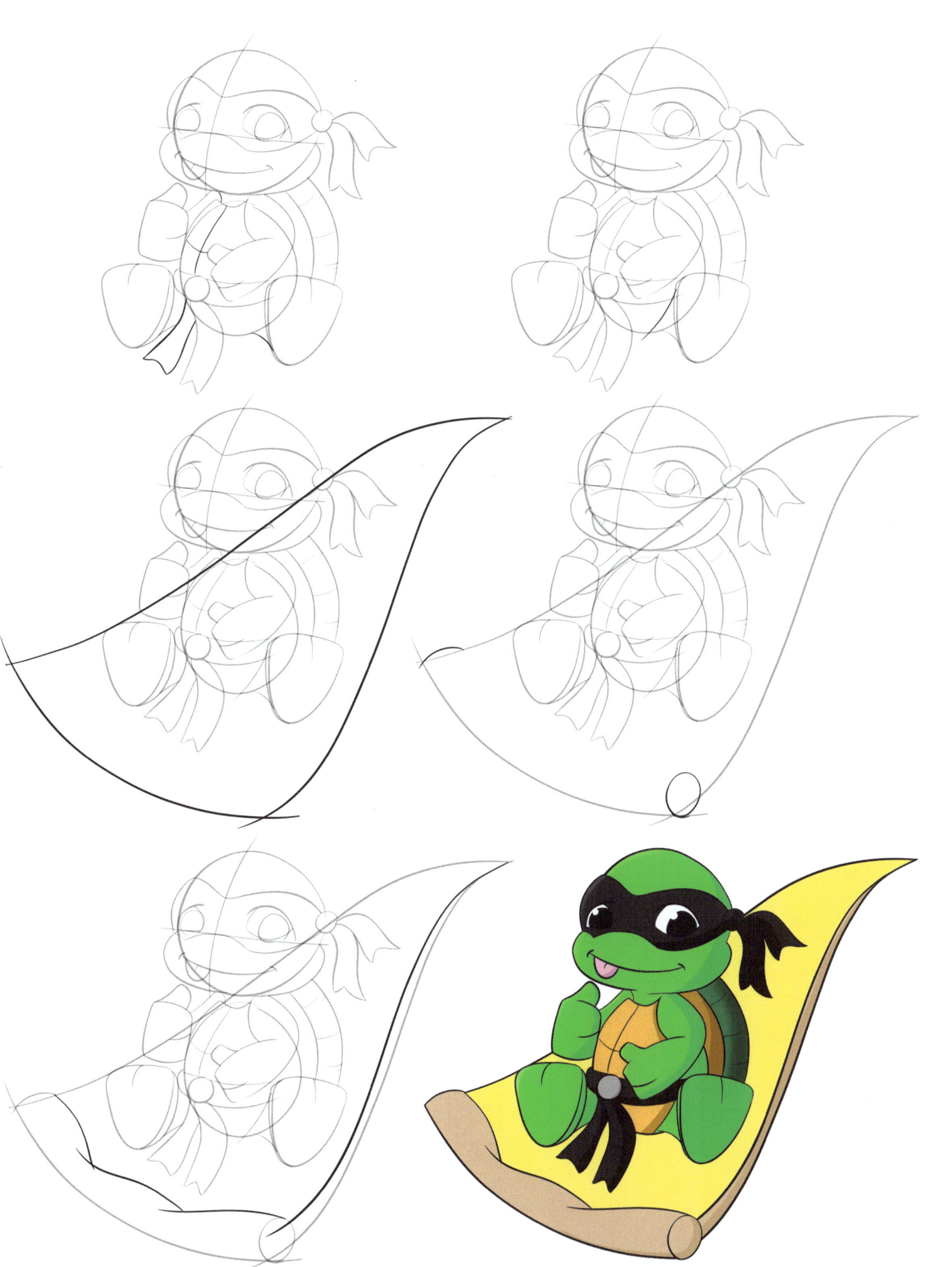

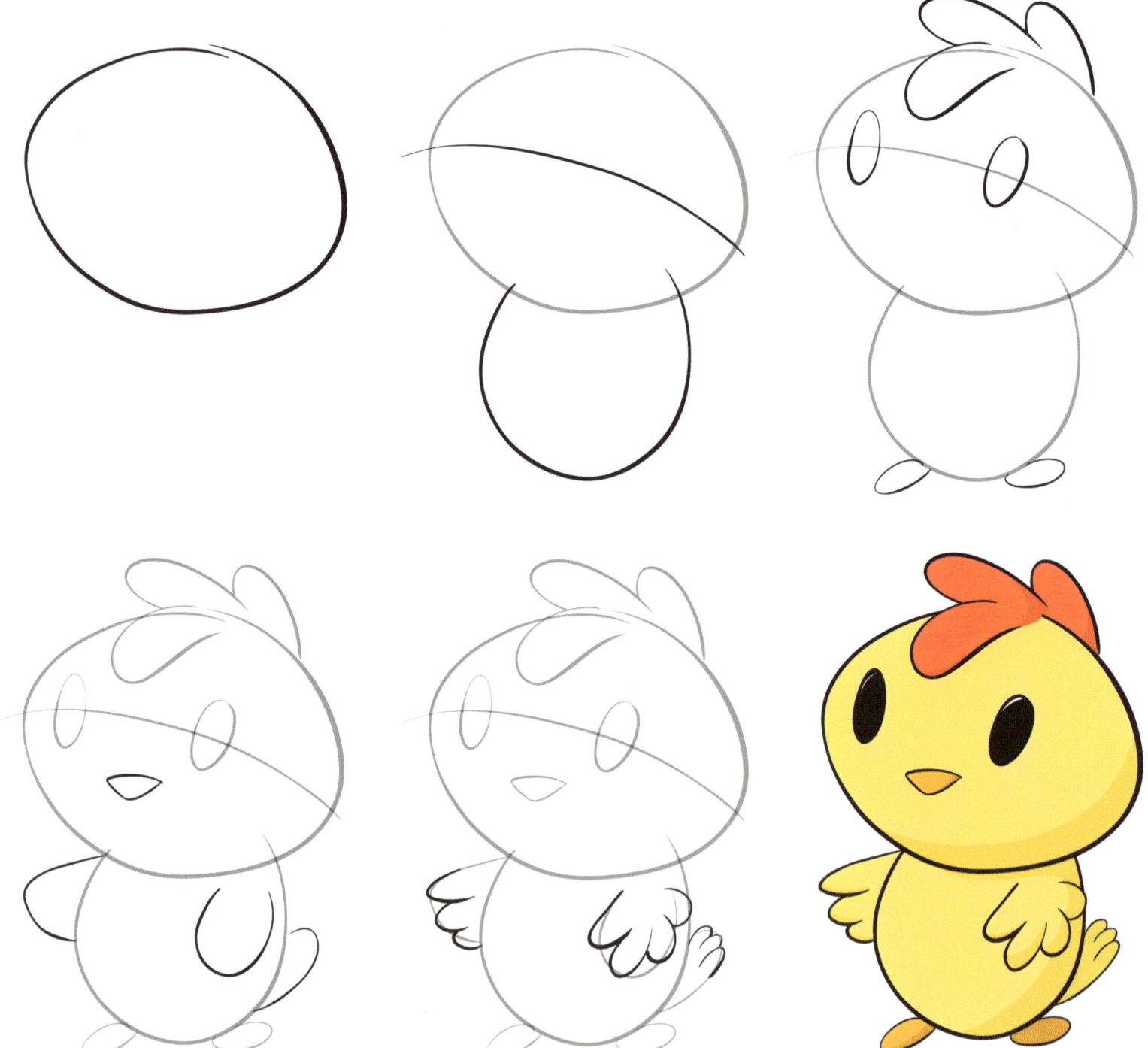

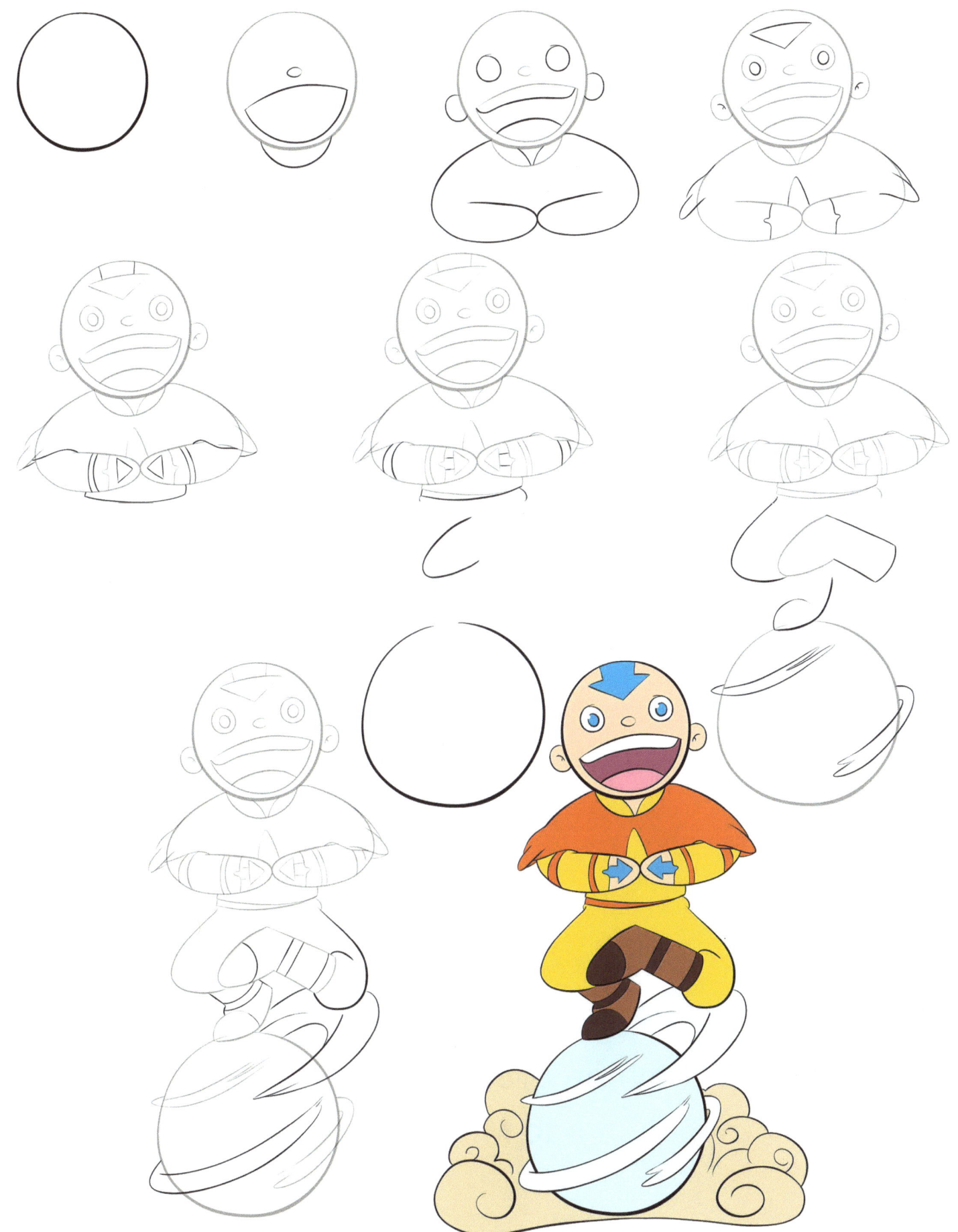

Remember: Drawing is about having fun!

Don't worry about making the perfect circle or square, just keep practicing. Don't draw just what is in this book, take what you've learned and create your own creatures and characters.

For other books and tutorials please visit

www.shawndurington.com

or

www.facebook.com/ArtofShawnDurington

Join us in our drawing group on Facebook:
Drawing with Melvin and Me

www.ingramcontent.com/pod-product-compliance
Lightning Source LLC
Chambersburg PA
CBHW040409220526
45473CB00004B/1177